JUST EAST OF SUNDOWN

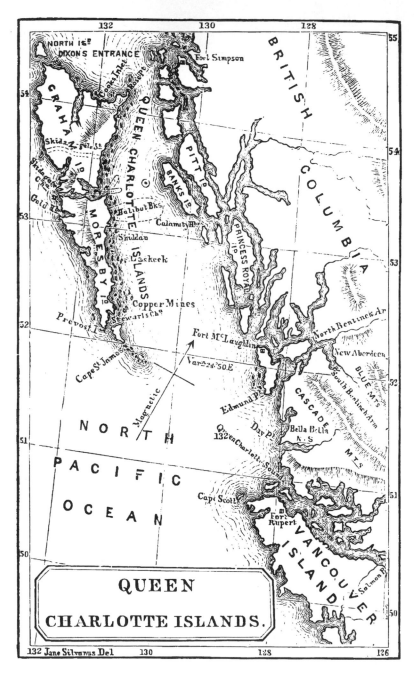

The Queen Charlotte Islands. (FROM POOLE, 1872)

JUST EAST OF SUNDOWN

The Queen Charlotte Islands

by

Charles Lillard

Horsdal & Schubart

Horsdal & Schubart Publishers Ltd.
Victoria, B.C., Canada

Cover photograph by Al Harvey, The Slide Farm, Vancouver, B.C.

This book is set in Galliard Book Text.

Printed and bound in Canada by Hignell Printing Limited, Winnipeg.

Canadian Cataloguing in Publication Data

Lillard, Charles, 1944-
Just east of sundown

Includes bibliographical references and index.
ISBN 0-920663-34-6

1. Queen Charlotte Islands (B.C.)—History 2. Queen Charlotte Islands (B.C.)—Description and travel.
I. Title.
FC3845.Q3L54 1995   971.1'12   C95-910281-7
F1089.Q3L54 1995

CONTENTS

To Chris Leding
Who told me about the Eagle at Howkan

THE CALL OF THE ISLANDS

I

ISLANDS. ISLANDS. The lure of islands, the mystery and the mystique of islands; lost islands, holy islands and those islands found only on pirate maps. Look up "Islands" in the Library of Congress or the British Museum and instantly there is reading enough for a lifetime. If you require something more personal, turn to the great islanders: Odysseus, Robinson Crusoe, Paul Gauguin and John Millington Synge working on islands poised at the edge of the known world, and Robert Louis Stevenson—an islander and a creator of islands.

But look as you will in those great libraries, you will find little about the Queen Charlotte Islands. They are not included in lists of famous islands. No artist or poet has made them immortal. Historians and geographers have paused there to move characters and names about in a desultory fashion, and then passed on. Nothing on the islands attracted explorers, nor did they draw hunters and sports fishermen; there was no big game and the real lunkers—the salmon that broke records—were caught farther south and north at easier-to-reach places. None of the first settlers left memoirs of their days on the islands, either, though the daughter of one early-day family became the islands' first historian. Before the 1960s, the only people to write books about the Queen Charlotte Islands were miners, missionaries and scientists, all of whom were more interested in the Haida than the islands.

Even those who lived on the nearby mainland of British Columbia traditionally showed little interest in what lay westward. In his account of his 1946 trip to Vancouver Island and the Queen Charlotte Islands, Ed Ricketts ("Doc" in John Steinbeck's *Cannery Row* and co-author of *Between Pacific Tides*) wrote: "None of the office people of the SS Co [steamship company] have ever been to the Charlottes and, as it develops, none on this particular steamer which is just taking us to Prince Rupert for trans-shipment there. Ticket seller here particularly, knowing me from reading correspondence regarding the trip, washes his hands of the whole affair. Asked me first why in Heaven's name we wanted to go to such a place, then if we knew anyone there, and ends up by saying, 'Well, all I can do is to sell you the tickets.' " [1]

Few of the trans-Canada travel books written since the 1880s have done more than note the islands. Even the individual travellers who later wrote books about their time in British Columbia rarely made it out to the Charlottes. And when they did, their visits left them befuddled, like Mediterranean sailors who've heard the Sirens: Vera Kelsey was no exception. An international traveller and novelist, Kelsey visited the islands in 1957 and wrote *British Columbia Rides A Star* the next year. Her comments are full of the beauty of the place and equally chockablock with the sort of confusion alleged to be caused by siren song.

"Neither Cumshewa Inlet's green waters nor the heavily frosted and forested mountains through which they wind into northeast Moresby Island are the beautiful innocents they appear. Dangerous fixed and shifting rocks lurk beneath the surface. And the rocky, machete finger of a 'half mountain' pointed righteously heavenward is a visible reminder of what they can do. A few years ago a pre-dawn earthquake sucked the other half into the inlet, created great fissures in surrounding areas, and panicked the population lest the entire island sink into the sea." [2]

There were two logging camps in the area, Aero and Moresby, but so ugly were they that none of the passengers went ashore. In both places Kelsey was struck by the youth and cleanliness of the loggers who came aboard to sit (a euphemism for drinking?) in the ship's lounge until the ship sailed.

She was impressed by Sandspit and its new airport and the equally modern village—"white homes, duplexes, and quadruplexes for the personnel." But if the irony of seeing a slice of suburban North America transplanted in toto to this island wonderland slipped by her, the sight of Sitka spruce ("30-foot logs, three and four feet in diameter") being shipped to pulp mills did not. "They will be towed," she wrote, "to Ocean Falls, Powell River, even to Vancouver, to be ground into newsprint or possibly into pulp for the carton containers of soft drinks the *Coquitlam* left in wholesale quantities at each port!" [3]

Moments later the hypnotic spell of the islands was back; Kelsey tells us: "Just when the prophecy, implicit in modern and noisy Sandspit, of development to come for the Queen Charlottes will be realized is as uncertain as the dates for Old Masset's funeral feasts. The islands are believed to be rich in minerals. Coal, gold and oil are known to be there. Graham's plateau offers good farming and grazing lands. Commercial forests cover Moresby and most of the 150 small islands. Some of the finest halibut fishing banks in the world lie off their Pacific seaboard. Other commercial fish and shell-fish inhabit their shore waters." [4]

Few visitors to the islands appear to have considered the paradox that lies behind such rhapsodies. Until recently these writers could, in one breath, talk lovingly about the scenery and wildlife of the islands, and then, without even inhaling, talk just as enthusiastically about the economic potential of the place. If even one of these writers ever wondered how mines and sawmills, oil wells and canneries could be developed without destroying the landscape, the question is not on record.

This incongruity has existed from the very beginning of history in the Queen Charlotte Islands. Beauty was noted and appreciated— then raped by fur traders, miners, loggers, settlers and hippies. Today, despite all the environmental reforms, the inherent contradiction of loving the islands for their beauty and isolation continues as the tourist trade in the islands expands.

What this paradox proves, ultimately, is that distant and magical as they are, the Queen Charlotte Islands have not escaped the ravages that swept industrial and post-industrial Canada. Until the 1970s, at every step, their story is but a continuation of mainland history. What happened after that is different, but to understand the significance of these changes one has to turn back the pages to the mid-1770s.

Written history begins in the islands in 1774 and lasts less than a week. It begins again in 1785 and continues intermittently—chronicling only a few days at a time—until 1833. History does not stir again until the discovery of gold at Mitchell Harbour in 1851. Some ten years later a mining engineer arrives to look for copper and remains for a few months. He is followed by other visitors, traders whose time on the islands is both incidental and spasmodic, leading up to the arrival of Reverend W.H. Collison of the Anglican Church in 1876. A few years later, with the arrival of industrialists and settlers, modern history begins in the Queen Charlotte Islands. Until the 1970s, island history will consist of the life-and-death struggles of logging and fishing, mining and oil exploration, agriculture and civic initiative.

History in the islands is the record of a disastrous Imperialistic policy of exploration and exploitation that began in the 1780s and continued on into the 1980s. Judging from what has taken place on the islands of western Ireland, the South Pacific, Greece and Italy, in the coming years tourism in the islands will leave its own peculiar mark on the Queen Charlottes. Regrettably, this mark will probably prove no more attractive than those left by logging and mining.

Yet, in spite of all of this history, the islands remain a place of wonder in the popular press, and are elsewhere referred to as the Haida Islands, the Canadian Galapagos, the Land of Hidery, the Misty Isles, Gwaii Haanas and Islands at the Edge. Paradoxically, all of these names are as inaccurate as they are accurate. To explain this is to explain how this book gained its present form.

II

Although this is my first complete book about the Queen Charlotte Islands, large portions of three of my previous books—editions of earlier accounts—were about the islands. One way or another I have also written a good deal of journalism about the place. But even after all of this work, visits, and endless hours of talk with friends who had—or would—live in the islands, I failed to see anything special about the islands and the Haida.

My first encounter with the Haida and their islands was one Saturday in 1949, when my father took me to the Field Museum in Chicago. If he had to drag me away from the Northwest Coast exhibits that day, he made up for it by taking me back; then we moved to Southeast Alaska. There I grew up and later worked with men and women from nearby Haida villages—Edenshaws, Gunyahs and others whose names turn up repeatedly in the history of the Queen Charlotte Islands. But it was not until I moved to British Columbia that I encountered people who believed the islands and the Haida to be absolutely unique. This was an eye-opener. Having grown up in the midst of several hundred miles of islands, most of which were identical to the Queen Charlottes, I found this view parochial, as it was, but the time was ripe with such views; it was the heyday of Canadian nationalism. Nevertheless, the notion of the singularity of the islands did not go away as did the nationalist fervour of the late 1960s.

Wherever I turned in my reading and writing about the Queen Charlottes, I encountered examples of what made the islands different—with the implication that this made them better, too—from the rest of the world. These examples ranged from stories of Haida superiority over the other coastal peoples, their huge canoes, and the even bigger spruce and cedar on the islands, to the isolation and natural beauty of the area, the gold and copper that might be found there, and the rare species of wildlife that existed nowhere else but on the Queen Charlotte Islands. True or not, these ideas, and many more like them, are the backbone to the most persistent and widespread geographical concept in British Columbia: that no place on the Northwest Coast is as extraordinary as are the Queen Charlotte Islands.

Exploring this concept offers an intriguing perspective of a truly remote area in British Columbia and the Pacific Northwest. And, yes, I have come to believe that the islands are unique, but not for the accepted reasons.

One evening soon after finishing the first draft of this book, I started piecing ideas together. Here is what I sketched out:

"The long-held, popular view of the islands' singularity is attributable to our adoration of nature, a Romantic view, which only works on a day-to-day level if nature has been made safe or civilized, or if it is observed from a distance—as from Vancouver and Victoria. Nature that has not been humanized is alien and, as Aldous Huxley has pointed out, 'occasionally diabolic'. Although Haida art is certainly not diabolic—as is evil or devil worship—it did originate at a time when the Haida believed in a plethora of characters that would have been considered diabolical in Europe until quite recently. And there is no doubt about it: the forms, characters and metaphors of Haida art are alien."

That was it. Brief as the assay was, it reminded me of the many turning points in island history I had encountered while writing the first draft of this book. This collision of the Wordsworthian view of nature and the Haida view of nature was another such point; one given shape by distance—our distance from nature and the traditional

Haida distance within nature—and this is what made the islands unique historically. It was as though the people who went there to exploit or settle had taken one step beyond the west; as though they had stepped into the east and lost their bearings. There, ideas conceived in Europe and carried across a new continent by waves of land-hungry people no longer sufficed. There, Europeans gave up the dream of pioneering and civilizing the land, and the Indians were triumphant. The Queen Charlotte Islands became the first place in North America where pioneers and businessmen lost their crusade of exploitation. Now I could write the second draft.

Historians may decide that this European turnabout, which gave the Haida the chance to reclaim their place in the world—a move that saved the islands—should be attributed to environmentalists and First Peoples' nationalism, and to economics and politics. But I do not think such a claim will be possible until someone makes a thorough study of the economic, spiritual, and cultural consequences of the great smallpox epidemic of 1862-63. Thousands died at this time and the survivors were demoralized to the point of inertia; research may show that it took the Haida 100 years to recover from the upheaval caused by this epidemic.

Today the Haida remain. The whaling stations are gone; mining and logging are disappearing, and the military is almost gone. Great chunks of the islands are parks or ecological reserves and one island is a World Heritage Site. Soon some island areas will be as wild as they were 100 years ago.

Viewed from this angle, the story of the Queen Charlotte Islands may be one of the few real success stories in Canada. No one writer can presume to write all of this story, but each can provide details and perspectives. I am proud to have tried to do this.

Charles Lillard

CHAPTER ONE

CEREMONIAL TIME

PREHISTORY

IN THE Queen Charlotte Islands "time immemorial" began about 9,000 years before the present at a place now known unofficially as Skoglund's Landing on Graham Island. In many respects this is not a particularly early date. Island-hopping in the Mediterranean was well underway by this time, as it was in that area generally known as the South Pacific. The Queen Charlotte Islands' date might, on the other hand, be considered incredibly late, for a maritime group of hunter-gatherers not unlike the Haida reached Australia and New Guinea around 40,000 BP.

Generations of students have been taught that the first Americans entered the New World via Beringia, a land bridge that has connected Alaska and Siberia during the various ice ages, when ocean levels were much lower than today. It is thought that, during the last of these ages, an ice-free corridor stretched through the centre of British Columbia, Yukon and Alaska. Using this route Asian migrants entered the New World, and their ancestors, hundreds of generations later, reached the Pacific Coast. So claims traditional wisdom. But what if there had existed a northern maritime culture, one that crossed the Bering Strait by water and remained on the coast, generation after generation, working its way southward into the myriad islands that form and protect the Inside Passage?

Until recently, such an idea would have been given little credence. No record of such a culture exists, and coastal conditions 10,000 BP were thought to have been too extreme for human migrations. The truth is: no one is sure what the conditions were 10,000 or 12,000 BP. It is known that there were people on the west coast of Peru 19,000 years ago and people south of the Great Lakes 16,000 BP. Given these dates, it is likely that people, moving down the coast a few miles every generation, from one protected area to another, would have reached the Queen Charlotte Islands by 9,000 BP. As the Bering Strait can be crossed by kayak and umiak in summer, and winter crossings on the ice are possible for months on end, the ancestors of the people who reached the islands may not have crossed into the new world on a land bridge.

For some years scientists have speculated that a few of the highest points on the Queen Charlotte Islands were not glaciated during the last ice age. Certain types of life could have survived on nunataks, the summits of mountains that remained ice-free. Now scientists are saying that much of the coast may have been ice-free even before the rest of British Columbia was emerging from under hundreds of feet of ice 10,000 to 12,000 BP. Evidence of one protected area or refugium, which is probably 16,000 years old, has been located on the east coast of the islands.

It is quite possible that the first people to arrive on the Queen Charlottes were not even maritime—merely people who had reached the coast and continued on foot to what are now the Queen Charlotte Islands, a few families at a time. A land bridge may have connected the islands and the mainland. This has been doubted, yet Beringia existed and now a few scientists are wondering if a similar bridge did not connect Japan and China during this same period. A bridge consisting of nothing more than lakes and marshland between the mainland and the islands is not beyond the realm of possibility. Newspapers reporting a recent discovery of a submerged island near the Queen Charlottes by Heiner Josenhans, an oceanographer with the Pacific Geoscience Centre, described the find as a Garden of Eden for the Haida. In this view sea levels in Hecate Strait were so much lower 10,300 years ago that the Queen Charlottes would have been within easy boating distance of the mainland. Much of Hecate Strait, which now separates the two areas, would have been dotted with islands at that time. Some of these islands must have been quite large, for exploratory work by the PGS indicates that many of them contained freshwater lakes, lakes now 120 metres below sea level.

How the first people or proto-Indians reached the islands is not as tantalizing a question as who they were? Nothing is known of these people except that they used stone tools. That will likely be all that is ever known, as 9,000 years ago the sea levels on the islands were 30 metres below today's. Whatever else these early people left behind has been covered by water for thousands of years.

In time these people died out or migrated elsewhere and were replaced by maritime hunters and gatherers who crossed Hecate Strait by boat. Archeologists think these hunters moved on or were overcome by a people who became the Haida some 5,000 BP. These people—Haida means "people" in their own language—began to emerge from what is almost the total darkness of this period of prehistory about 5,500 to 3,500 BP. But these dates are arbitrary; some scientists believe that the Haida or proto-Haida may date back to the very beginnings of human life on the islands. That the traditional Haida lifestyle is old seems incontestable: in 1987 a Haida village possibly 4,000 years old was discovered on a small island off the east coast of South Moresby.

After 5,000 BP middens began to build up on the islands. Middens are the garbage dumps of North American Indians. On the Northwest Coast they consist of heaps of clam shells, bones and other similar cast-away matter. Overgrown and forgotten until modern science rediscovered them, they are now a major window into the past of the people who created them around their villages.

About the time middens were appearing, the way of life in the islands was changing. Contact with the mainland was re-established, sea levels were close to what they are now, rivers and their deltas had stabilized, and the red cedar began to flourish. It is thought that the seasonal runs of salmon and eulachon into island and mainland rivers and streams might have been established at this time. As both fish would become staples for the Haida and other coastal peoples, as well as for land and sea mammals, this period was the end of migratory life on the coast. In these years, the Haida, like other Northwest Coast peoples, left their ancient hunting-and-gathering way of life behind and began developing a way of life that was so complex it has amazed everyone who has come in contact with it. Even after a hundred years of intensive study, Haida culture has yet to give up all of its secrets.

THE CULTURE OF THE COAST

The coast between Coos Bay, Oregon, and the rock-strewn and windy shores of Yakutat Bay, Alaska, was traditionally the homeland of more than a dozen Indian peoples. All of these, from the Eyak living elbow to elbow with the Chugach Eskimo, to the Athapaskans of southwestern Oregon, were culturally similar but linguistically and physically distinct. Experts agree that so few were the similarities between the arts and industries, customs and beliefs of these people and their neighbours, that the people of the Northwest Coast created a culture that can be considered unique and independent of other cultural groups in North America.

Still, no matter how similar the people of this area were, there remained cultural differences that made each unique. The Tsimshian were traders, the Nootka whalers, and the Haida were famous canoe builders. Sometimes, as with the Nootka on the west coast of Vancouver Island, there was little uniformity between the people of one village and the next. These differences make it clear that the development of each cultural sub-group was a slow process, dependent on trade and war with their neighbours, with each generation adding details until there existed the cultural mosaic encountered by the Spanish explorers and priests in the 18th century.

For generations of anthropologists and travellers, the Northwest Coast was the area stretching from Puget Sound, Washington, to the general area of the present-day villages of Haines and Skagway, at the head of Lynn Canal in Alaska. This coast is a long, narrow reach rarely more than 120 miles wide and not quite 1,000 miles long. It is this geography that shaped the destinies of the Haida people of the Queen Charlotte Islands.

The mountainous coast with its dozens of bays and sounds, passages and inlets, and literally thousands of islands, reminded many earlier tourists of Norway. The area is temperate, heavily wooded, and generally wet, the average rainfall in some areas being the heaviest in North America. As travel in this area was virtually impossible except by boat, all the coastal peoples were expert boatmen. Each family or village had a fleet of canoes; there were canoes for war, fishing and hunting, and others for the women and children. Bad weather could isolate even the closest villages during the winter. The generally mild weather that is consistent in this area during the rest of the year made travel on the inside coast, along what would become known as the Inside Passage, reasonably easy, protected as this waterway is from the Pacific Ocean by a chain of islands.

Just as canoes made the Inside Passage a waterway for trade and war, the inlets reaching into the heart of the Coast Range opened up the interior. The Fraser and Skeena were the major rivers on the coast between Puget Sound and Lynn Canal, but rivers like the

Stikine, which debouches into the Inside Passage near Wrangell, Alaska, and the Bella Coola and Nass rivers in British Columbia, were hardly less important. On all these rivers there have been migrations downstream and upstream; some Haida families may have used the Stikine River to reach the coast, and at least one Tlingit group from Alaska moved up the Skeena River. None of these suspected or known migrations into greener pastures were invasions: they were intrusions, neighbours feuding over property and taking advantage of each other's weaknesses. In the case of the Haida who migrated into Tlingit territory in Southeastern Alaska, the right to the territory was taken as payment for Tlingit having accidentally killed an elderly Haida chief.

Although the coastal waterways were hospitable to seasoned travellers, no one—contrary to many published opinions—travelled far; there was no need to. The Kwakiutl and Nootka on Vancouver Island traded and fought, but they had nothing to offer the Haida or Tsimshian, who were trading partners; so it went north and south. Thus the coastal peoples remained relatively isolated until the large-scale movement of Europeans into their homeland in the 19th century.

Another side of this "homogeneous group" was revealed by the anthropologist Diamond Jenness. "The isolation of their home and their dependence on the sea made the Haida great voyagers, and, as is commonly the case with maritime peoples, keen imitators of the tribes with which they came into contact.

"In their dug-out canoes they raided the mainland [in historical time] as far as Sitka in the north, and to the lower end of Vancouver Island in the south. Naturally they encountered most frequently the Tlinkit and the Tsimshian, and it was from these tribes that they borrowed most extensively. They copied with indifferent success the basketry of the Tlinkit, and derived from the same source most of their shamanistic paraphernalia and songs. Their phratries bore the same names as the Tlinkit phratries, Raven and Eagle, and were similarly divided into a number of clans, with subdivisions into family groups or 'houses' each governed by its own chief. From the Tsimshian, with whom they traded canoes and sea-otter skins for Chilkat blankets and the oil of the oolakan or candle-fish, they derived the majority of their dance songs, and the beginnings of a secret society that the Tsimshian had themselves taken over from the Kwakiutl." [1]

A Canadian government publication earlier in the century went into patronizing detail about these peoples. It considered the Haida,

Tlingit and Tsimshian more adaptable to modern ways of life and showing much less religious fundamentalism than did many of the tribes south of Vancouver Island, to whom the settlers considered the Haida superior. It was widely claimed that of all the coastal tribes, the Haida, both in Alaska and British Columbia, were the finest artisans.

THE HAIDA

Although physically the people of the Northwest are by no means homogeneous, which the explorers and traders realized more than 200 years ago, the Haida are like the others belonging to a variation known as the American Indian form of Mongoloid. The Tlingit, Haida and Tsimshian, who share the coast of Southeastern Alaska, the area around the Skeena River and the Queen Charlotte Islands, were historically thought of as a broad-faced group, who were distinct due to their height, relatively long arms and legs on a shorter than expected body, with a correspondingly broad face.

In one of the best general descriptions of how everyone on the coast dressed, the anthropologist Franz Boas wrote: "The natives of this region go barelegged. The principal part of their clothing is the blanket, and this was made of tanned skins or woven of mountain-goat wool, dog's hair, feathers, or a mixture of both. The thread is spun on the bare leg and by means of a spindle. Another kind of blanket is made of soft cedar bark, the warp being tied across the weft. These blankets are trimmed with fur. At the present time woollen blankets are most extensively used. At festive occasions 'button blankets' are worn. Most of these are light blue blankets with a red border set with mother-of-pearl buttons. Many are also adorned with the crest of the owner, which is cut out in red cloth and sewed onto the blanket. Men wear a shirt under the blanket, while women wear a petticoat in addition. Before the introduction of woollen blankets, women used to wear an apron made of cedar bark and a belt made of the same material. When canoeing or working on the beach, the women wear large water-tight hats made of basketry. In rainy weather a water-tight cape or poncho made of cedar bark, is used.

"The women dress their hair in two plaits, while the men wear it comparatively short. The latter keep it back from the face by means of a strap of fur or cloth tied around the head. Ear and nose ornaments are used extensively. They are made of bone and of abalone shell. The women of the northern tribes wear labrets." [2]

The usual picture of the Haida as a sea-going people, something like the Vikings of legend, who dominated their neighbours is quite false. Most reports are based on legend and rumour; students of the Haida tend to be romantics who dream of a pristine past that never existed. They forget or ignore the most impressive feature about Haida culture: that it was certainly the most adaptive on the coast, perhaps in North America. The only major general distinction that can be drawn between the Haida, and their nearest neighbours the Tlingit and Tsimshian, was their homeland. But the Queen Charlotte Islands did not isolate or protect the Haida from the Tlingit and Tsimshian; both raided the islands as often as the Haida attacked mainland villages. A less obvious, and almost ignored, distinction is the origin of the Haida and their language.

One traditional view of the Haida was that they had been there since Raven created them. Raven, cultural hero—a transformer figure who travelled the coast creating and destroying at a time when the animals lived in villages as the Haida later would—is said to have created the islands because the world was then covered by water and he wanted a place to rest. So, by beating his wings against the water, and turning the spray into rocks, he made himself a roost. Later, according to one popular story, he created people in a clam shell. One traditional story tells of the Haida descending the Skeena River and sailing out to the islands, where they displaced an earlier people. Another suggests they descended the coast from the Aleutians.

All of this may be possible. Whatever their origin, they are a people with a language that appears to bear no relationship to any other language in the world. Although living in widely separated villages, the Haida spoke one language. Historically, there are three recognizable divisions of Haida territory: the Northern Haida consisting of the Kaigani Haida in Alaska, with major villages at Kasaan and Hydaburg, and the people of the northern coast of Graham Island, Masset being their centre. The Central Haida had only one remaining village of importance—Skidegate, on the north shore of Skidegate Inlet, which separates Graham and Moresby islands. And then there was Ninstints on Anthony Island, the only permanent village of the Southern Haida, which had been abandoned by 1890.

ENVIRONMENT AND GEOGRAPHY
The Queen Charlotte Island world of the Haida is an adze-shaped archipelago stretching northwest some 156 miles from Cape St.

James to Langara Point. From Langara Point to Rose Point, which forms the head of the adze, this archipelago is less than 70 miles wide; add another 50 miles to this imaginary line and the eastern end rests on the mainland coast, a little south of Prince Rupert. More than 150—some say 200—islands make up this group. Graham Island is the largest with an area of 2,485 square miles. Next is Moresby Island, some 1,060 square miles in extent, and separated from Graham by narrow, tide-swept Skidegate Channel. Louise Island, the third in order of size, contains 124 square miles. After this come Lyell, Kunghit, Burnaby, Talunkwan, Tanu, and Ramsay islands. Together, the Queen Charlotte Islands encompass some 3,840 square miles lying between 52 and 54 degrees North, and 141 and 134 degrees West.

Physiographically, the islands are composed of the Queen Charlotte Lowland, the Skidegate Plateau, and the Queen Charlotte Ranges. The southern border of this lowland stretches from Beresford Bay on the west coast of Graham Island to Sandspit on the east coast of Moresby Island. Usually described as an extensive area of low relief, this is a muskeggy area supporting red and yellow cedar, lodgepole pine, hemlock, and spruce. Except for two broad rises with elevations of 600 and 1,200 feet, and the 2,100-foot-high Argonaut Plain that fills the Cape Ball-Masset-Rose Point triangle, the lowland lies below 500 feet in elevation.

Skidegate Plateau is an ever-widening corridor reaching west from Skedans Bay on Moresby Island to Frederick Island on the outside coast of Graham Island. It averages slightly more than 2,000 feet in elevation, dropping to 1,500 where it borders the lowland. On this border the vegetation tends to be alpine or muskeg; elsewhere the plateau is the islands' most heavily timbered area.

The Queen Charlotte Mountains are an exposed and extremely rugged backbone stretching from Rennell Sound to Cape St. James. Although the average height of these mountains is anywhere from 1,500 to 3,000 feet (thus a good deal lower than the mainland mountains, the profile of which frequently rises above 8,000 feet), several peaks—including Mount Kermode and Mount Needham—are about 3,500 feet high, and others may exceed 3,700.

Haida geography did not include the interiors of any of the islands, so far as is known. For one thing, the dense forest and miles of muskeg made travel difficult; for another, there was no particular reason to venture away from the coast. Occasionally they did do so, but only when travel by water was possible, such as when hunters made seasonal canoe trips into the marshes and ponds dotting the Queen Charlotte Lowland to hunt ducks and other waterfowl.

When working with the Tlingit at Angoon in the 1950s, the American anthropologist Frederica De Laguna observed: "Almost all the place names which we secured referred to bodies of salt water (bays, coves), the streams that enter it, islands, points, rocks on the shore, or to mountaintops visible from the water. Had we been able to go inland with a guide we might have secured names of hills, tributary streams, etc., but it is probably significant that not one of our informants mentioned such specific features of the land, except for a few lakes in which the sockeye salmon spawn.

"The Tlingit world is," she continued, "essentially the ribbon of the shoreline that winds along the indented coasts of the islands and fiords. Its parts are linked by boat routes across open water. Only in certain places does the world expand with arms that run inland up the streams to some lake or to a trail that links the headwaters of two bays." [3]

This is the Homeric geography of maritime hunters, travellers and warriors. To visualize the Haida world is to see something similar to a marine chart, and one early *Coast Pilot* provides a notion of the Haida geography between Masset and Virago Sound, west of Masset Sound on Graham Island. "The coast between these two places is everywhere low and wooded, with occasional open grassy spaces, differing from the coast east of Masset, in being rocky or covered with boulders. No wide sandy bays occur, and the points are mostly of dark low rocks. The trees along the shore are not of great size and are interspersed with occasional grassy spaces." [4]

It does not sound like a hospitable shore, and that is what would have mattered to travellers. But when the *Pilot* goes on to state that there are wide fields of kelp in the vicinity and the "water is shoal far off shore," hunters and fishermen listened. This might be a haven for otter, sea birds, fish and crabs.

Rugged as the islands may be, the weather is generally mild. Except in the mountains there is rarely snow; it is rainfall that can be daunting. The annual rainfall on the west coast of the islands is twice that of any place in Canada east of the Rockies, but is similar to that on the outside coast of Vancouver Island or the Prince Rupert-Bella Coola area.

TOWNS AND TOTEMS
The Haida lived in towns and at one time there were supposedly as many as 126 of them, but historically only some 20 may have been actual winter villages, i.e. towns where families and groups gathered

to spend the winter months. There were eight southern villages: Skidegate, Haina, Cumshewa, Skedans, Tanu, Ninstints, Kaisun and Chaatl; and nine northern villages: Masset, Kayang, Yan, Hiellen, Kung, Kiusta, Dadens, Yaku and Tian. Dadens on North Island was the northernmost of the villages, and Ninstints on Anthony Island was the southernmost. Ninstints was also a west-coast town, as were Tian, Chaatl and Kaisun. Except for Masset and Skidegate, which are still Haida towns, none of these existed into the 20th century. Several, in fact, were abandoned as early as the 1850s.

The village of Ninstints on Anthony Island at the southern tip of Moresby Island is now a World Heritage Site, and the best known of the ancient village sites. Anthony Island, so small as to be hardly visible on most large-scale maps of British Columbia, is both an ecological reserve and a provincial park.

Originally the village's name was Sga'nguai, which means either Red Cod Island or Red Cod Island Town. But as the chief of the village was called Nan Stints (One Who Is Two) of the Raven clan, the first explorers used his name when they referred to the village. The same thing happened at Skidegate, Skedans and Cumshewa, so that now their original names are forgotten or only half-remembered.

Little is known of the history of Ninstints. The first European to leave a record of visiting the area was Captain George Dixon of the *Queen Charlotte*, after which the islands were named. This was in

Village of Masset in 1878. (COURTESY GEOLOGICAL SURVEY OF CANADA)

1787. The first visitor to offer something of a portrait of the people and the place, in 1789, was Robert Haswell, who served as second and then first mate aboard Robert Gray's *Columbia*.

Haswell was curious and went ashore and encountered "a fortified Rock which I suppose in case of invasion is their place of refuge it was purpindicular about forty feet high the top was flat with about twenty yards wide it was inacessable on all sides except by an oald rotten lader that was erected by its side this for they call Touts [a fortified retreat] and when their northern neighbours come to molest them they pout their Women and Children up thare while they fight the battle they say it is their custom to eat their vanquished enemies and said it was excellent food."

There is no evidence that the Haida ever practised cannibalism, either in prehistoric or historic times. However, they did have rituals that might have been misconstrued as cannibalism and heads were taken as trophies.

Before the ship sailed, the "natives brought us for sale a number of excellent hallibut and Boiled gulls eggs," and Haswell noted that our "intercourse with the natives while we lay in this Port was on the strictest Friendship they indeed pillaged aney little trifling thing they could find a good opertunity to take unobserved but as we took no rash meens with them it never interrupted our trade." [5]

There are no early descriptions of Ninstints. The harbour facing the village is tiny, and Anthony Island is exposed and small, so this was not a place for sailing ships, whose officers and crews knew nothing of the area. A visitor to Ninstints in the 1950s left a sparse but definitive account of the appearance of the place. The description makes it clear why the Haida chose the site.

"The site of Ninstints village is remarkably well sheltered....Tucked in a tiny bay half-way along the eastern (or lee) shore-line, it is protected from the winds and waves of the open Pacific by the whole breadth of the island, and from easterly winds and swells by a small rocky islet which sits just off the bay, sheltering it almost completely. At low tide the bay goes completely dry. At high tide, no matter what the weather, it is a smooth pond several feet deep, entered through a narrow passage around the south end of the islet. The rocky northern channel is not navigable. The beach and floor of the bay consist mostly of smooth pebbles, although near the entrance, beds of boulders and low rock outcroppings jut from the bottom. In at least one place, directly opposite the entrance, boulders have been moved aside to form a canoe runway.

"Landward from the beach, the ground rises gradually, then is broken by a vertical north-south wall of rock faces, which in some places form cliffs scores of feet high, and which is indented at intervals by fissures and caves," the visitor continues, and in doing so provides a basic description that might fit any of the known village sites on the Queen Charlotte Islands. "Extending south from the bay for a few hundred yards is a meadow-like flat, which is bordered on the west by the rock cliffs, on the east by a high wooded knoll (which helps to shelter the village from southeasters), and on the south by another rocky beach.

"The houses stood around the rim of the bay, facing the entrance. Following the curve of the southern half of the bay is a terrace about 20 feet high, and most of the houses were located in a single line close to the first crest of this terrace." [6]

Most of the known Haida villages were located in similar protected areas and were made up of only one row of houses; larger towns are probably mythical. Kung, at the head of Virago Sound, may have once had two rows; Skidegate—originally The Place of the Stones, whose chief was Skidegate, Son of the Chiton—was made up of two partially overlapping rows of houses; Cumshewa, Skedans and Tanu had houses that sat between the beach and the long row of houses higher up on the foreshore.

"A basic description that might fit any of the known village sites": Skedans, 1878.
(COURTESY GEOLOGICAL SURVEY OF CANADA)

Village of Skidegate in 1878. (Courtesy Geological Survey of Canada)

It has been claimed that the giant cross-beams and supporting posts of the Haida houses, and all the carvings that seemed like embellishments or ornaments, were a source of wonder and speculation to American and British fur traders, but there is little indication of awe in even the earliest descriptions of these houses. The French explorer Etienne Marchand, captain of the *La Solide*, surveyed Parry Passage separating Graham and North islands in 1791. His account of his time in the islands provides one of the first and best descriptions of a typical Haida house.

"The form of these habitations is that of a regular parallelogram, from forty-five to fifty feet in front, by thirty-five in depth. Six, eight, or ten posts, cut and planted in the ground on each front, form the enclosure of a habitation, and are fastened together by planks ten inches in width, by three or four in thickness, which are solidly joined to the posts by tenons and mortises; the enclosures, six or seven feet high, are surmounted by a roof, a little sloped, the summit of which is raised from ten to twelve feet above the ground. These enclosures and the roofing are faced with planks, each of which is about two feet wide. In the middle of the roof is made a large square opening, which affords, at once, both entrance to the light, and issue to the smoke. There are also a few small windows open on the sides. These houses have two stories, although only one is visible, the second is under ground, or rather its upper part or ceiling is even with the surface of the place in which the posts are driven. It consists of a cellar about five feet in depth, throughout dug in the inside of the habitation, at the distance of six feet from the walls throughout the whole of the circumference. The descent to it is by three or four steps made in the platform of earth which is reserved between the foundations of the walls and the cellar; and these steps of earth well beaten, are cased with planks which prevent the soil from falling in. Beams laid across, and covered with thick planks, form the upper floor of this subterraneous story, which preserves from moisture the upper story, whose floor is on a level with the ground. This cellar is the winter habitation." [7]

This was a large house. Chief Weah's Monster House at Masset was only 54 feet by 55, but it had three levels: the bottom level was built around a firepit; next came a narrow tier running around the four sides of the firepit or central housepit; and above that was a wider tier where people slept. Most houses consisted of only one level with a firepit below ground level, when the ground made it feasible; such houses were large enough for one family and its extended family unit—slaves, poorer relatives, visitors.

Like so much else in their daily lives, the Haida houses were built of cedar, a light but strong wood that is easily worked with even the most primitive tools. The uprights or posts were left in the round, though frequently embellished with totem figures or designs. The beams were sometimes left in the round, sometimes split from larger logs and squared, either by hand with an adze or by further splitting with stone—later iron—wedges. The planks covering the walls and sometimes the roof were split from trees or cants (previously squared logs). If the roofs were not planked—each plank overlapping the next as with shingles—slabs of cedar bark were used in a similar fashion.

All the totems in museums and parks were carved sometime after mid-nineteenth century, and the majority may not be more than a century old. "Native technique," Marius Barbeau stated, in terms that have been claimed, but not proven, to be wrong, "reached its fullest development in the last century, and after 1860. It hinged upon European tools, the steel axe, the adze, and the curved knife, which were made in imitation by the natives or were traded off in large numbers to them from the days of the early circumnavigators, that is, after 1778. The lack of suitable tools, wealth, and leisure in the prehistoric period precluded elaborate structures and displays. The benefits accruing from the fur trade at once stimulated local ambitions; they stirred up jealousies and rivalries and incited sustained efforts for higher prestige and leadership. The overmastering desire everywhere was to outdo the others in ingenuity and wealth, power and display. The totem pole came into fashion through the rise of these ambitions, fostered mostly by the fur trade. It became the best way of announcing one's own identity in the commemoration of the dead, the decoration of houses, and in the perpetuation of traditional imagery. The size of the pole and the beauty of its figures proclaimed the fame of those it represented." [8]

Etienne Marchand left one of the earliest descriptions of a totem. "This door, the threshold of which is about a foot and a half above the ground, is of an elliptical figure, the great diameter, which is given by the height of the opening, is not more than three feet, and the small diameter, or the breadth, is not more than two. This opening is made in the thickness of a large trunk of a tree which rises perpendicularly in the middle of one of the fronts of the habitation, and occupies the whole of its height; it imitates the form of a gaping human mouth, or that of a beast, and it is surmounted by a hooked nose about two feet in length proportioned in point of size to the monstrous face to which it belongs. Over the door is the figure of a man carved, in a crouching attitude, and above this figure rises a gigantic statue of a man erect, which terminates the sculpture and the decoration of the portal. The head of this statue is dressed with a cap in the form of a sugar-loaf, the height of which is almost equal to that of the figure itself. On the parts of the surface which are not occupied by the capital subjects, are interspersed carved figures of frogs or toads, lizards, and other animals." [9] This was a house frontal pole and the hole was the entrance into the house.

Other types of poles, though some are hardly more than decorated posts (to which the origin of the totem can be traced), were house posts, on top of which the house beams sat; commemorative or memorial poles, raised in honour of a dead chief or noble; and mortuary poles, wherein coffins were built to hold the body of the person commemorated by the pole. Although welcoming figures and grave markers are sometimes referred to as totem poles, they are actually statuary. Thinking back to the 1870s, Collison wrote in his memoirs that "the Haida custom was to issue invitations early each year, and to assemble as many of the tribes as possible to one point or village for the dance and potlatch. It was generally arranged some weeks previously which town should be the rendezvous, and due preparation was made to receive and entertain the guests. Sometimes in a large village there would be several totem poles carved and awaiting erection. Of these, one or more would be mortuary totems for deceased chiefs, and the others crest totems erected by the chiefs or leading men to signal their succession to a title or chieftainship." [10]

Despite the ceremony, totem poles rarely stood for long in their original locations before rotting off at the base and falling down, where they were disregarded and left to rot. The best of those still standing in the deserted villages after the 1880s were stolen or sold to collectors. None were cut down or burned by order of missionaries.

THE YEARLY CYCLE

Towns like Cumshewa and Ninstints were not year-round villages. Come spring the families in every village went their own ways, to fish, hunt, and gather berries and wild plants, in the areas traditionally owned or used by each group. The groups did not return until fall. One late 20th-century version of the Haida year has it consisting of 12 months: Bear-Hunting Month, Goose Month, Noisy Goose Month, Migratory Geese Month, Food-Gathering Month, Berries Ripen Month, Ripe Berries Month, Salmon Month, Cedar Bark for Hats and Baskets Month, Ice Month, Bears Hibernate Month, and Snow Month, all of which may seem to conform too neatly with European months. A list of the months published almost a century earlier is surprisingly similar to this list: Goose Moon, Bears Come Out of Hibernation Moon, Laughing Goose Moon, Foreign Goose Moon, Moon of Flowers, Berries Begin to Ripen Moon, Berries are Ripe Moon, Salmon Moon, Cedar Bark Moon, Salmon-Smoking Moon, Ice Moon, Bear Paw the Ground for Roots Moon, and the Standing Up to Relieve Nature Moon (i.e. the time when it's too cold to squat).

The major times to gather food were March, when herring eggs were gathered; May, when people collected black seaweed; June, the time for catching red salmon; July, for picking berries of almost every kind; and October, when people collected dog salmon eggs.

The first major event every year for many Haida was the eulachon fishery at the mouth of the Nass River. The eulachon—also spelt oolichan and oulachan—is a small, smelt-like fish that comes in from the sea every spring to spawn in a few of the coastal rivers. These fish are so oily that, once dried, they were used as torches. Pioneers inserted wicks and used them in the place of candles; thus they became the famous candlefish. Most of the tribes had their own eulachon rivers, but the Haida and various Tlingit and Tsimshian

villages did not. For their eulachon they had to go to the Nishga—
People of the Nass River—an independent and powerful Tsimshian
people. After a winter of living on dried fish and berries, everyone
needed grease or oil. The Nootka on the west coast of Vancouver
Island hunted whales for oil; the Haida, Tlingit and Tsimshian fished
or traded for eulachon.

"To this maritime centre another element was added by the arrival
of the Tsimshian and Tsimshian-Tlingit from the upper Skeena
River. These people had as much contact with the interior as with the
coast. Thus they became the middlemen of the interior trade, one of
immense value involving large canoes, loaded with 80 cases, or close
to 2,000 kg of eulachon oil each." The Reverend W.H. Collison, one
of the first Europeans to live year-round with the Tsimshian,
continued: "For centuries the eulachon fishery on the tidal waters
had attracted the tribes from all quarters. From the interior, hundreds
of miles distant by trail, the Indians thronged, carrying their effects
on sleighs drawn by their dogs or by themselves (as they generally
started early in the year while the snow was deep) in time to reach
the river in time for the fish, which usually arrive about the middle of
March. They brought with them also fur, the proceeds of their
hunting expeditions, with which they pay the tribes resident on the
river for the right to fish, and for the use of their nets and for shelter
in their fishing lodges during the season." [11]

Nowhere on the coast did so many people gather to trade, at the
same time processing the five to nine tons of eulachon each family
required annually. The rent paid by the interior people was only part
of a trading system, as Collison observed. "These furs were principally marmot and rabbit skins, generally sewn together to form rugs
for bedcovers or robes. Marten, mink, and bear skins were also
tendered and accepted. But not infrequently when pressed by famine,
which was not unusual among the inland tribes, they handed over
their young children in barter for food. These were in turn passed to
the Haida as part payment for their canoes, which were so necessary
in their hunting and fishing.

"When Fort Simpson was established by the Hudson's Bay
Company in 1834," Collison went on, "the Tsimshian, attracted by
the advantages afforded for trading there, removed from their old
villages at Metlakatla and on the Skeena and established themselves
around the fort. To this point also the Haida came every year to
exchange their furs, principally the sea otter and fur-seal skins, for
guns, ammunition, and blankets. Few such visits passed off without a

fight, as the Tsimshian were jealous to see the Haida possessing themselves of the white man's weapons and they regarded them as intruders." [12]

This was a later aspect of spring trading. Before the arrival of the Europeans and their goods, which upset the centuries' old trading patterns, everyone traded peacefully. They had to. The Haida needed oil and salmon, having no eulachon streams of their own and only a few large salmon streams, and the Tsimshian needed canoes.

In June 1874, Collison witnessed the arrival of a Haida trading party. "The fleet consisted of some forty large canoes, each with two snow-white sails spread, one on either side of each canoe, which caused them to appear like immense birds or butterflies, with white wings outspread, flying shorewards. Before a fresh westerly breeze they glided swiftly onward....These were the Masset Haida, who were famed for their fine war canoes. They have always been the canoe builders of the northern coast." [13]

Canoe building was part of the yearly cycle of the Haida. This cycle revolved, according to area and tradition, from the winter months that were spent in the houses and villages already described, through the early eulachon fishery, which would have been replaced in many of the isolated Haida villages by seal hunting. Early in May, which the Haida knew as the Month of Flowers, families started moving out to their summer camps to gather seaweed. This was also a time for halibut fishing, now that the weather was calmer; herring were netted when possible and their spawn, considered a luxury, was also gathered, by anchoring spruce boughs in bays where herring were known to spawn. It was also the time to gather the inner bark of the red cedar, which was used for weaving and sewing.

In June the people moved again, this time to their salmon-fishing camps. Berry-picking was another full-time activity, as was collecting shellfish. During these months the Haida ate various plants fresh; these plants were also boiled and stored in boxes to be eaten later with eulachon oil. Berries and seaweed were also stored for winter use, as were dried salmon and halibut.

The remainder of the summer was given over to the salmon fishery. After the salmon season was over in October, the men turned to hunting bear and a variety of sea mammals and seafowl. Winter was another important time for gathering shellfish as the weather made hunting and fishing difficult; men carved during these months and women wove. It was a time for potlatches and the dances put on by the secret societies.

Canoes were carved during the early spring months. Usually the large cedars needed for these projects had been felled and prepared in the fall and then left to dry. Months later, when the weather began to improve, the logs were moved to the beach worksite and the technician and his crew began work. Work on totems was done in a similar fashion, and there were almost as many types of totems as there were canoes.

There were hunting and fishing canoes, war canoes—these are the huge vessels of history and legend—women's canoes, and canoes for children and general use. None of these were sea-going canoes. The Haida did not hunt whales as did the Nootka; like the Tsimshian and Tlingit, they travelled north and south along the Inside Passage, more than 90% of which is protected from the open ocean by hundreds of islands. They were all a riverine people in the way they used the coast and waterways. In fact, according to the missionaries, the Haida were not even particularly sailor-like in their thinking.

One aspect of the notion of sea-going canoes requires explanation. When travelling from camp to camp, or camp to village, the people took along their house planks, the posts and beams being the only parts of the house that were stationary and permanent. Since it was difficult to tow these planks, they were laid across the hulls of two canoes; atop this the gear and luggage were piled. It was also a comfortable place to ride. The appearance of canoes connected by this planking led various writers to compare them to the catamarans of the South Pacific.

That the development of the Haida canoe, sometimes worth as much as one slave in trade, had reached the point it had by the 1770s may be because the Haida had iron before the other coastal peoples. It is equally possible that having iron tools made it possible for the Haida to carve totems similar to modern poles. The first historic evidence of totems comes from the Queen Charlotte Islands.

CHAPTER TWO

SPIRIT HELPERS AND PROCLAMATIONS OF PRESTIGE

To UNDERSTAND the Haida at the time of contact with Europe, one would have to understand winter in the Queen Charlotte Islands. It is surprising, considering the number of books about various elements of Northwest Coast life, that no book about coastal winters has been written. The only book that touches on the isolation, weather, and that overwhelming feeling of being caught between sea and forest is Rockwell Kent's *Wilderness*, an autobiographical account of winter on an island hundreds of miles north. Should a specific book on coastal winters be written, it could be the introduction to a spiritual history of the Haida.

Winters in the islands 300 years ago are almost unimaginable. Most late 20th-century Europeans have no basis on which to build, image after image, a world lived within a town consisting of no more than a dozen houses, which is, except for brief trips made by visitors and traders during spells of good weather, totally isolated from nearby villages. There are only 300 to 400 inhabitants—slaves, commoners and nobles—and very little to do. Slaves do most of the work for the nobles; the commoners tend their fires and their children and eat. Most years, there is more than enough food for everyone, so, even if the weather allows, which it usually does not, there is no need to hunt or fish. That is summer work. There are few potlatches. Those famous feasting and gift-giving ceremonies held by the neighbours of the Haida—and by the Haida in the 19th century—were for the most part a late aspect of Haida culture, as were the winter dances that kept other coast people occupied for weeks at a time.

There is rain, there is wind, the rising and falling tides, and the raucous noise made by the village ravens and crows as they scavenge and gossip. Even during the occasional lulls the sound of dripping water is everywhere. The scene is one out of the west of Ireland, or the northernmost islands of Scotland, in centuries past. Inside the huge houses it is always dusk; the people nearest the fire at the heart of the house turn to their elders and storytellers in such weather. There they hear tales as had their parents and grandparents back hundreds of generations. Echoes of this world are to be found in the stories recorded by Jacob and Wilhelm Grimm and in the Norse sagas. The forest is dangerous: it is inhabited by witches and goblins, elves, cannibals, mad people. The sea, too, has its creatures that are best avoided.

Stories are told endlessly and everyone listens, for they live on a narrow edge of land between the sea and forest. Not a man nor woman in the house has escaped encounters with creatures at sea like the Supernatural Halibut or Dogfish Mother, or unexplainable voices in the berry fields behind the village, which may have been coming from the Crab of the Woods. Everyone is a member of the Eagle or Raven clans. They listen for explanations, for familiar stories that remind them of their ancestors or the history of their clan, and, like everyone who has listened to storytellers, they listen for the pure enjoyment of being entertained.

In such an atmosphere, carving, giving physical form to characters in stories, would have been a natural pursuit. Man the image-maker has always attempted to interpret visually what he has seen, heard or experienced. For the Haida, with soft and easily worked red cedar everywhere about them, nothing could have been more likely. It must be remembered, though, that artists rarely emerge from a void. In this case, between the storyteller and the carver stood the person who had a foot in the so-called real world of the storyteller—the Haida historian—and the visionary world of the artisan—the Haida artist. This man or woman, for on the Northwest Coast gender was no barrier for those who wished to bridge the distance between the world they knew and the world of the spirits, was, depending on whose spelling is taken into account, the *ska-ages* or *sa-ag-ga*, the shaman.

SHAMANISM

Shamanism is a religion practised by men and women of the Pacific Northwest Coast, parts of Asia and Northern Europe, Siberia and the North American Arctic, which enables them to heal the sick, foresee events, and communicate with the spirit world. The main difference between the shaman—one who practises shamanism—and the priest—one educated to stand as mediator between people and their gods—is that there was no body of knowledge that the shaman must learn. Generally, in North American literature, the term "shaman" is synonymous with "medicine man" and, until recently, "witch doctor".

The coastal shaman was a person who, while on a quest for guardian spirits, encountered magical beings. These entities chose the person they possessed to be a medium or channeller, and using that person's voice they spoke to mankind. When the spirit was in control, control was complete, to the point that if a Haida shaman's spirit or supernatural being was Tsimshian, the shaman spoke that language, even though he or she had never heard Tsimshian in their life. Although evidence suggests the Haida were not as dependent on shamanism as were their neighbours, at least in the 19th century, they held certain of their shamans in tremendous respect. One Haida shaman buried at Image Point at the southeast corner of Graham Island was known as Linagit Tla, a Tlingit phrase that has been translated as Mother of the People. The term "mother" reflects the term "town mother" and "town master," another name for the chief of the town.

The only educated Europeans known to have worked side-by-side, so to speak, with the Haida shamans—at least shamans whose traditions had not been contaminated by civilization—were the Anglican missionaries. The first to reach the islands, W.H. Collison, had little to say about the shamans in his memoirs. And when he does mention them, it is to chortle: I won, you lost. Once in the late 1870s, on hearing that there was another outbreak of smallpox in Alaska, Collison obtained vaccine. He then called a number of chiefs (among the Haida there were three types of chiefs: house, family, town) and elders together, hoping to persuade them to allow him to vaccinate them. But they were not having any of it; finally, in desperation, he vaccinated himself, and that was enough for one chief, who remembered the last epidemic to hit the islands. But for Collison vaccination was more than a medical necessity. It would not only protect the Haida from their worst enemy, disease; it would, he believed, give him "another victory over the sorcery and superstition of the necromancers." [1]

Although everything that is known about the Reverend Collison suggests intelligence and goodwill, the man appears to have completely misunderstood the role of the shaman. Necromancy is based on communication with the dead and in practice is a type of divination that incorporates the remains of the dead, or parts of those remains, in its ceremonies. Certain shamans that Collison encountered on the islands may have been involved in some sort of necromancy, but it is highly unlikely.

Less than ten years after Collison had brought Christianity to Masset, Charles Harrison, another British missionary, took a longer look at the traditional role of the shamans and concluded they "occupied the unique position of prophet, sorcerer and physician" amongst the Haida.

Some of what Harrison had to say about the shamans sounds too Christian to be believed (e.g. the Haida worshipped a supreme deity who stood for good and was known as Lord of All Things), his other observations are so bald that there is no reason to doubt them. "As may be readily understood the functions of the medicine men and the witches have rarely been fully appreciated by European residents and were often looked upon merely as jugglers. There did not appear to be any association whatever between the members of this profession, and each practised his art singly and alone whenever a demand was made for his services and the proper fee was paid. In fact, instead of the medicine men working together harmoniously, there was a great rivalry between them, and one tried to do more wonderful acts than the other." [2]

Harrison's description of the individuality of the shamans can be projected across the Haida world. Each family in each house in each village went its own way every spring. The three types of chiefs stood independent of one another and there was no one chief to whom every Haida looked. The family chief's power was such that he might refuse to participate in raids led by the town chief. This same independence was to be found in each village: each village was a complete and self-supporting unit.

Shamanism among the Haida did not seem to be as important as it was among the Tsimshian, and, to a lesser extent among the Tlingit. If this is true, and there is no way of knowing for sure, it may be due to the Haida having only recently borrowed the particular Northwest Coast form of shamanism from their neighbours. Or the lack of interest may be attributed to a lack of knowledge on the part of the people who have written about the Haida; after all, like poetry itself, shamanism was learned and perfected in private and performed among the uninitiated. Each time the shaman approached the spirit world, he or she went forth "to encounter for the millionth time the reality of experience and to forge in the smithy of my soul the uncreated conscience of my race." [3]

It is often claimed that, as Christianity took hold of the Haida imagination in the 1870s, shamanism began to slide from sight under the gaze of the church and was not missed. Possibly, but this does not explain why shamanism became a leitmotif for Haida carvers at about this time.

These artists have been called the Ska'ages Carvers. Most of them worked with argillite—"a compact argillaceous rock cemented by silica and having no slaty cleavage"—and were among the first generation of Haida carvers to leave their visions writ large in Queen Charlotte Island history.

Argillite carving of a shaman. (FROM DEANS, 1899)

DOORS OF PERCEPTION

More interesting than these carvers, few of whom are known by name, is the still unanswered question: why the immediate (and from all we know it was as sudden as it was unexpected) interest in the shamans on the part of the carvers? Was it because Christianity was phasing them out? Was it because the shamans were the most dramatic and the most "Haida" of the subjects available to these island carvers? Or was it homage that inspired these little-known carvers?

The answer is probably a synthesis of the above. But since these carvings, particularly those by the mysterious William Dixon, are as dramatic as anything done by Charles Edenshaw and Bill Reid, two of the greatest of the many great Haida artists, no generalized answer is going to be suitable.

It is difficult to look at the Ska'ages carvings as simplistically as have many of the people who have written about Haida art. The Haida world in the Queen Charlotte Islands was, as was the Tlingit in Alaska, a maritime world. But unlike the Tsimshian and Tlingit, the Haida had no way of escaping their environment: the Tlingit and Tsimshian had close ties to people living at the headwaters of the Stikine and Skeena rivers, and the Kwakiutl and Salish had similar mainland connections, while the Nootka or West-Coast People were closely related to the Makah on the Olympic Peninsula. True, the Haida of the Queen Charlotte Islands had relatives in Alaska, but those people had moved north in what were the final moments of unrecorded time in the islands, probably in the early 17th century. The Haida were alone.

Late in the 19th century the Haida artists may have mourned the passing of their shamans because they realized that with their passing a door to nature had closed. The shaman—visionary, seer, poet, healer—was a source of inspiration and solace to whom the Haida had turned, much as Europeans turned to English Romantic poets like William Wordsworth, and German artists like Caspar David Friedrich. The Haida turned to nature in this instance for, despite all its horrors, it was the one place they were not alone. It was their library and museum and art gallery. Inside this landscape the shamans were the guides and through them the carvers received their inspiration.

ONE LANDSCAPE: THREE VIEWS

I

Today, the concept of the islands is that of a wilderness wonderland with abundant fishing, hundreds of species of birds, and so many deer that people have been known to get out of their cars and shoo them off the road, but this is largely a 20th-century notion; it has been fostered first by the government to encourage settlers, now to sponsor tourism. And each step of this attempt to Europeanize the islands was another remove from the world of shamanism, the spirit of the islands.

This "wilderness wonderland" view began in the 1860s when an amateur anthropologist in Victoria started visiting the islands and published numerous mythological-anthropological pieces. Besides gathering the curious impression that Haida was pronounced Hidery, he picked up enough material for a Haida village display at the 1893 World's Fair in Chicago. His name was James Deans and his renderings of tales the totems tell was apparently one of the hits of the fair. It was also the first sympathetic international press for the Haida.

In 1899 the Archives of the International Folk-Lore Association published Deans' *Tales from the Totems of the Hidery*. In it he provides a view of the islands, probably the first and best view most 19th-century readers would ever be offered. "On the west coast," wrote

James Deans, at left, with Haidas at Masset. (FROM DEANS, 1899)

Deans, "the Queen Charlotte group are mountainous and covered with timber. The eastern parts are level, with large tracts of open land, some of which is swampy, owing to the streams being filled with log jams, which prevents the bottom lands from being drained. The west coast is very wet, while the east is dry. The climate owing to its humidity, is often chilly, but not extremely cold....all sorts of vegetables may be grown there, fruit trees seem to do well. As for cereals I can only say that wheat, barley and oats have been tried as an experiment and found to ripen, peas do well, so do potatoes, turnips and carrots. Small fruits grow abundantly on the hill sides. Wild strawberries, large and luscious, grow in rich profusion on the new made lands left by a receding sea on a rising land." [4] Deans says nothing about the islands as the Indians knew them; he sounds like a representative of the local board of trade, were there one.

II

Francis Poole, a miner and engineer who was the first European to live on the islands, learned about the island landscape the hard way. The experience he later described in his book about the islands would be re-experienced by thousands of hikers, prospectors and land-seekers.

"After breakfast we set off in the direction of a high mountain, situated in the interior of the island, intending, if possible, to ascend to the summit, and secure one of the many hundreds of eagles' nests which I could plainly discern through my field-glass. Though the distance to the base of the mountain was only about three miles, so dense a bush separated us from it, that we found it absolutely impracticable to proceed more than two. Indeed, the last half-mile I performed alone, my Indians having given it up as 'unco uncanny,' to borrow a phrase from yonside the Tweed. They aver that I penetrated into the interior further than any Indian has ever gone. This does not surprise me, considering their natural dislike to exertion of any kind. They plead in excuse that the game is too scarce, and the under-bush too obstructive and dangerous, to offer them sufficient inducement. As I was forced to go back myself, I must admit their plea to be a reasonable one." [5]

An equally hard-eyed view of the island landscape was shown in 1906, when Charles Sheldon, a big-game hunter from the United States, arrived on the islands in search of the elusive, maybe mythical, Queen Charlotte Island caribou. Later, he described the landscape through which he hunted so unsuccessfully as miles of muskeg meadows, swamps, swampy lakes, unnavigable rivers and high salal. In his weeks on Graham Island he was plagued by rain and storms, never once cocked his rifle, saw no living mammals—and certainly no caribou; he had, however, seen a variety of inedible birds such as crows and ravens. But this was not enough for Sheldon; he had to make comments typical of most Europeans of that period.

"Those who read this narrative will wonder," Sheldon wrote six years later, "how it could be possible that these Indians had never seen a caribou on the island. I also still wonder at it. The Indians have always gone into the interior along the rivers, to set traps for bears or martens, also to get trees for their canoes, and occasionally they have crossed the island to the west coast. One had been accustomed to go over to Lake Jal-un to trap, and had even constructed a house there. But, except along the rivers, they seldom went far back in the woods. Since there are no deer or other game animals on the island, except the bear, which they only trap, the Haidas have never been big-game hunters." [6]

III

Most of the Haida, continued Sheldon, were afraid to go far back into the interior of the islands, due to their superstitions. According to him their traditions alleged that all types of "monsters and hobgoblins" haunted the forest. As seen earlier in this chapter, Sheldon was right, and this landscape of the Haida imagination, which remains unexplored by Europeans, may point to another role played by the shamans. Already identified as seer, visionary and healer, this profession may have also had those who were teachers. In fact, it is feasible that the people identified as shamans formed a professional middle class among the Haida. This would help explain why intelligent observers such as the Reverends Collison and Harrison did not agree on the role played by the shamans. So little is known about the Haida shamans that this suggestion must remain hypothetical, but it is not a "maybe" that they were the seers and poets with direct connections to the spirit world. Teachers in this situation, given the Haida necessity to concentrate all their energies on subsistence at least six months of each year, may have created a certain number of sea and forest creatures not as objects of fear and horror, but as symbols to guide the Haida in their daily lives.

Without clearly established fishing and hunting rights, and without the fulfilment of obligations—the payment of which usually took the form of food or trade goods—the Haida faced potential starvation daily. There had to be rules and rules usually have stories behind them, and the shamans were the storytellers.

CEDAR AND STORY

Cedar had been available to the Haida for at least 4,000 years. It is not only soft, it is buoyant, and durable if not used roughly. It was a wood that the Haida would utilize almost to the same extent as the Plains people used the buffalo. Among other things, the bark was used for clothing and matting; the roots for baskets; the withes for ropes and thread; and the wood—in the round and split into planks—was used to build houses; canoes were dug out and shaped from logs; and the straightest cedar trees were used for totems. Whether or not the Haida relationship to the cedar on the islands went further than this is another unexplored subject.

Elsewhere on the Northwest Coast the spirit of the cedar was dealt with very carefully and its powers were not maligned. These powers were said to be both healing and spiritual, which suggests the tree may have been sacred to the shamans, or their class, which would have included technicians, teachers—and carvers. As the traditional Northwest Coast shamans were those who communicated with nature and brought information to this world, nothing would be more likely, or traditional, than the wish to describe and to see what the shaman had encountered. In other words, the artist brings a dream or vision to life. One story told of what happened to Natsilane, a Tlingit carver, whose killer whale came to life and sought to avenge his creator, whose brothers had abandoned him.

Natsilane's was the first killer whale, and as a benefactor to the Tlingit it became Killer Whale, a clan crest or emblem. The Haida possess the Raven-finned Killer Whale legend in which a whale chief is accompanied by a raven. According to informants the Killer Whale was the emblem of the people of Tian, the only west-coast village on Graham Island. From his mother this informant inherited a variety of crests: the Hat of Abalone Pearls, the Grizzly Bear (which was Tlingit), the Killer Whale, and the Raven, which was the crest of the clan to which he belonged.

Judging from the story of Natsilane, and what little can be found between the lines in similar Haida stories, the carvers in Haida society lived as close to the world of nature as did the shamans. If so, both the carver and the shaman would have had close links to Raven, whether or not they belonged to families bearing that particular crest.

RAVEN'S WORLD

For many the most interesting spirit in Haida mythology is Raven. Were the geography not all wrong, this might be the same raven that Noah sent from his ark to scout for dry land. That Raven was turned black for his sins—for not returning to Noah, because, having found carrion, he settled down to feast—and the Haida raven was turned black for stealing the moon. Historically, Raven was sacred to Apollo, to Odin, and, it is said, to King Arthur; this is one of the reasons for the presence of the ravens who live on a royal budget at the Tower of London. As all of these figures were shamanic in origin and became divine, or semi-divine as in the case of King Arthur, this is another reason to suspect that the Haida shaman is a much more complex and important figure than heretofore outlined.

Prehistorically, from Siberia to Vancouver Island, Raven was not only a major figure in the spirit world, he was in daily life the symbol of the arbitrariness of life. On the Northwest Coast Raven was the crest of one of the two great clans, the Ravens. Ravens and Eagles. It is thought by some that the Eagle crest was a late development, perhaps borrowed from the Tlingit, who had adopted the crest from the two-headed eagle on the Russian flag. Historically, every Haida man, woman, child, and slave belonged to one or the other of these clans, and every village was divided between Ravens and Eagles. It was a necessity: for an Eagle to marry an Eagle was incest, no matter how distant the family ties might be.

Raven of the Queen Charlotte Islands was at different times a transformer, a trickster and a cultural hero. Dozens of collections of stories have been written about him, all based on various Northwest Coast myths, and all of them sanitized for children. In the original tales Raven was always curious, always greedy, and usually completely without shame, morals or regret. Superficially, the closest modern parallel to Raven in North American folklore would be cartoon characters such as Woody Woodpecker, or Wile E. Coyote, or more specifically the crows Heckle and Jeckle.

The majority of published Haida stories about Raven are based on a series of stories originally told to the ethnologist John Swanton through an interpreter at Skidegate in the winter of 1900-01. He called the series *Raven Traveling*; most read like outlines, such as this one, the first episode in the cycle.

"Over this island, they say. Raven flew about. He looked for a place upon which to sit. After a while he flew away to sit upon a flat rock which lay toward the south end of the island. All the supernatural creatures lay on it like Geno', with their necks laid across one another. The feebler supernatural beings were stretched out from it in this, that, and every direction asleep. It was light then, and yet dark, they say." [7]

It helps to add details to this story. It was told by John Sky of Those-born-at-Skedans. If John Sky was telling the story in a traditional form—the way he first heard it told, "Over this island" undoubtedly refers to Louise Island on which Skedans is located; otherwise "this island" refers to Graham Island, where Skidegate is situated and where John Sky was telling the story to Swanton. In a footnote, Swanton claims "this island" refers to the Queen Charlotte Islands, an odd aside suggesting, as it does, that Swanton's informant either spoke Haida badly or did not know that there was more than one island in the Queen Charlotte group.

Geographically, knowing the identity of "this island" is important if "a flat rock which lay toward the south" be sought after. John Sky's traditional audience would have known the location of this rock, as the Haida had names for every landmark within their landscape. What emerges from "this island" and "a flat rock" is a type of shorthand. John Sky did not bother to tell Swanton details. Similarly, Swanton did not ask his informant for specific details. What, for instance, is Geno'?

Swanton's footnote describes Geno' as probably belonging to the Actinozoa, which he understood to be a class of Coelenterata. This would make Geno' sea anemones; but "with their necks laid across one another" hardly describes the appearance of sea anemones. It is possible, given John Sky's obvious lack of interest in the story, that he was talking about a rock where sea lions were basking.

One episode of the Raven cycle makes more sense than most. As Raven walked along the shore he saw a spring salmon that was jumping. After watching this for a few minutes, Raven called out, "Spring Salmon strike me over the heart." And that is exactly what he did, hitting Raven so hard he was knocked off his feet. Raven got up shaking his head just in time to see Salmon disappearing into the water.

Then Raven built himself a stone wall just above the tide and another, running parallel to the first, a few feet above the first. Having finished these walls, Raven called out again, "Spring Salmon strike me over the heart."

Quick as a flash he did so, but this time the walls were between him and the water. He managed to knock down the higher one, but he was still slapping against the first wall when Raven got his breath back. Smiling, Raven picked up a club and beat Spring Salmon to death.

It was a big fish so Raven called to some nearby crows to help him eat Spring Salmon. Raven built a fire and put the fish on to cook and then lay back for a nap. He asked the crows to wake him when the fish was cooked, but instead they ate the fish. They stuck some of the remains between Raven's teeth, and when he awoke and found the fish gone, they told him he had eaten it. And sure enough, there was some fish between his teeth. But this did not fool Raven; he spat into the faces of the crows and said, "Future people shall not see you flying about looking as you do now." At that instant the white crows were turned black.

The story of Raven is only one of many myths that John Swanton collected. Most are not completely comprehensible, which must be one of the reasons that few collections of Northwest Coast myths utilize the Haida myths collected by Swanton. One small collection, *The Raven Steals the Light*, written by the Haida artist Bill Reid and the American-born poet Robert Bringhurst, is interesting, full of valuable information, and beautifully illustrated, but the stories are Anglicized. Even so, the last lines of the book are unsettling.

"The light the Raven stole has grown a little dimmer for all of us, but it still flickers in the houses of the people of Haida Gwai. And the old magic of the Islands, which were there even before mythtime, is

Pictograph showing Raven in the belly of Whale. (FROM NIBLACK, 1888)

still strong. The old ghosts will continue to haunt the land until new spirits can be born.

" There may be another time before anything was.

"But on the banks of some river somewhere, you may be sure, someone or something, even if it isn't us, is living, and the Raven and the Mouse Woman are wily enough to keep their stories going." [8]

One final note on Swanton's version of the Raven stories is necessary. At least two reasons for their disjointedness are possible: John Sky was probably a commoner and in a two-line introduction to a collection of Tlingit Raven stories, made by Swanton in 1904, he writes: "In olden times only high-caste people knew the story of Raven properly because only they had time to learn it." The possibility also exists that the Haida may have borrowed heavily from the traditional Tlingit stories and were in the process of "rewriting" them in the 19th century.

Another possibility is credible. Raven may have been sacred to the shamans and carvers—the story of Apollo suggests this was so elsewhere—which would mean his story was their story, and not told, or not told in great detail, outside their fraternities. Just as generations of young men and old have found themselves in the pages of Don Quixote, a shaman who cared to look found himself in Raven. With the passing of the shamans Raven disappeared. What was left was not Raven, merely the memory of Raven: details and story plots half-remembered by a few old men. The carvers mourned and carved their *ska'ages* in argillite.

A Totem Tells Its Tale

If the lack of information about Raven is now somewhat less inexplicable, what of the creatures who live within Raven's geography and Haida mythography? There is the one major collection of Haida myths gathered by John Swanton, but it lacks an index. Other collections of Northwest Coast myths, like Franz Boas' huge *Tsimshian Mythology*, contain a good deal that helps explain Haida myths, but it is difficult to locate and expensive. The great, two-volume compendium that Marius Barbeau put together and called *Totem Poles* is an endless source of information, but it, too, lacks an index. Most of this work is now 50 to 100 years old and badly out of date.

There are dozens of books and hundreds of articles about Haida culture and art, but nothing that can be used as a source book. Nothing more is known about the characters in Haida mythology than was known in the 1950s. Among the crests and figures listed in one inventory of poles that once stood at Skidegate are: Grizzly Bear, Wasko (Sea Wolf), Killer Whale, Mountain Goat, Three-Finned Killer Whale, Dogfish, Eagle, Raven, Sea Otter, Bear, Sea Grizzly Bear, Beaver, Moon, and a young Crow. The details that were carved in isolation, such as a whale's blow hole, are numerous, and undoubtedly many went unlisted. Each of these crests or details come from stories or events in Haida mythology or history.

The figures or symbols beg to be explained, and united with photos and drawings (and paintings in some cases) of the totems so that the work can be seen in context. It was long believed that totems told stories and could be read. This is as misleading as the contemporary idea that basically totems are little more than a visual reminder of a person's deeds and family connections. Traditionally, the crests on totems served as introductions to visitors, identified friends and foes, established family lineages, reminded all of great deeds of the past and were, like monuments in Europe and Asia, a way of keeping the past alive.

Impressive though they may be, some of the largest poles, erected late in the 19th century, reflected little more than bragging and bravado, and their creation and raising were supposedly financed with money certain Haida males obtained by pimping for the women in their families in Victoria, New Westminster and elsewhere. This is one version of the story. Another may be that these poles were erected as an offering to the spirit world to change history, if the connection between shaman-carver-family history and the spirits of the cedar (from which the poles were carved) has been established correctly. It is possible that by the 1880s or so the Haida, realizing that emulating the Europeans had been a mistake, were asking their ancestors and crest animals to come back.

Whatever the case, and the story may never be known for no one asked the right questions when the participants were alive, the fact that these creatures from the Haida bestiary were important individually and collectively is beyond doubt.

The classic definition of a totem or crest is Sir James Frazer's. It is, he wrote: "a class of material objects which a savage regards with superstitious respect, believing that there exists between him and every member of the class an intimate and altogether special relation." [9]

Raven, Wolf, Grizzly Bear, Blackfish (Killer Whale), Eagle, and Thunderbird were the outstanding crests of the North Pacific coast, according to Barbeau. Although they were used, he says, from Alaska to the Strait of Georgia, no one—meaning the coastal peoples themselves—made an effort to explain their significance and how certain families had obtained exclusive rights to use them. They were, Barbeau maintains, hereditary and taken for granted.

Clearly, the totem pole reflects the natural world of the Haida and, like a Renaissance painting, may be full of still readable imagery and symbols. In the Royal British Columbia Museum there is a copy of one totem, a house frontal pole, which the museum refers to as The Totem from Tanoo. Originally this pole was part of the House that Makes a Noise and it can be seen in many early photos of Tanu. It may also be studied in a watercolour by British Columbia's best-known artist, Emily Carr, who painted the original in situ in 1912. Her better-known oil painting, entitled "The Crying Totem", done in 1928, is a portrait of one of the figures on the Tanu totem.

There are nine figures on this totem; they are, top to bottom: Three Watchmen Wearing Ringed Hats, Eagle, Hawk, Hair Seal, Sea Chief, Frog, Man, Killer Whale, and Sea Bear. A book could, and one day will, be written about each of these figures. "Certain Haida chiefs," a staff member of the museum wrote, "had the right to display such figures [listed above] on the tops of their poles." [10]

These watchmen have supernatural powers and from their location are able to see bad weather approaching, and trouble, too; the height of their hats is a symbol of their owner's status. The watchman is not unlike Janus, the deity of gates, in Roman mythology. That four watchmen were often placed atop poles may also have something to do with the yearly round: Janus is sometimes portrayed with four faces because he presided over the four seasons.

Tanu, the common spelling today of Tanoo, was an Eagle town: that is, the ruling family belonged to the Eagle lineage at the time the town was abandoned. It was said to have been founded by Eagle families from Hlkia or Chicken Hawk Town on Lyell Island. As already stated, the Eagle was possibly Tlingit and Russian in origin, but there is one long and complicated story regarding families that once lived in the vicinity of the Naha River, near Ketchikan, Alaska. Supposedly these people were Tlingit with close ties to nearby Haida settlers. A leading family among these Tlingit, so goes one version of the story, tamed eagles and possessed stone statues of eagles. After a disruptive war drove them out of their homeland, one branch of the group moved to the Queen Charlotte Islands.

What it meant to have Eagle as a family crest may never be known for sure. It is claimed that a Tlingit Eagle (though Eagles

Watchmen atop totem poles at Skedans, 1878. (COURTESY GEOLOGICAL SURVEY OF CANADA)

were Wolves in most Tlingit territory) or Raven could move without worry through Eagle villages in the Queen Charlotte Islands and likewise a Haida Eagle was accorded similar privileges. How true this is, cannot be testified to; there are other stories where Haida Eagles in wartime were rescued from death by their Tlingit (or Tsimshian) clan members. But the rescued men, women or children were not given their freedom: instead, they were enslaved and sold back to their relatives at top-dollar prices. Who would know better what prices the market would bear than someone from the same clan?

The Eagle was, in the case of The Totem from Tanoo, the crest of the owner's wife's family or clan. And by Eagle the bald eagle is meant, a bird that once inhabited all of North America but is today restricted to isolated areas in the continental United States and most of western Canada, the Pacific Northwest and Alaska. There are some 9,000 eagles on the British Columbia coast, or 4,500 breeding pairs, and there are more of these on the Queen Charlotte Islands than anywhere else on the coast.

Scientifically, this eagle is not the American Bald Eagle (*Haliaeetus leucocephalus*) but a subspecies, the Northern Bald Eagle (*Haliaeetus leucocephalus alascanus*), which is identical to the American Bald Eagle except for size. The Northern Bald Eagle is slightly larger than its southern cousin.

Adults mate for life; they build nests in snags, large trees, or on cliffs close to their hunting ground. In the islands this means the nests are usually within a mile of the coast. Although their preferred food is carrion, eagles will hunt and fish if necessary; generally they find it easier to steal the fish caught by gulls and osprey. Those lucky enough to see this thief's mid-air performance will not soon forget the eagle's swooping dive, the startled bird dropping its fish, and the eagle doing a barrel roll and catching the fish before it has fallen more than a few feet.

Despite their totemic significance, the eagles were hunted by the Haida. These birds were not eaten, for along with seagulls and loons they are objectionable and inedible, but eagles supplied the feathers used on masks, and white eagle down thrown in the air and allowed to drift was a sign of peace, or peaceful intentions.

The next figure on The Totem from Tanoo is the Hawk. There are numerous species of hawks on the islands—including the peregrine falcon, osprey, sharp-shinned hawk, northern goshawk, red-tailed hawk, merlin and gyrfalcon—but as Hawk is sometimes referred to as Mountain Hawk, it may be a crest that originally belonged to the Gitskan of the upper Skeena River. There is also a possibility that this hawk, since the carver's idea is unknown, is not Hawk at all but Thunderbird. Among the Haida the symbolic representation of the two was often, if not always, identical. The reason for this is unknown.

Thunderbirds are ancient mythological beings, Asian in ancestry, and well known in the New World from Alaska to California, and from the Queen Charlotte Islands to the Eastern Woodlands. Everywhere, they are thought to be huge birds living in the mountains, who cause thunder when they flap their wings. On the Northwest Coast they caught whales as easily as osprey catch salmon. Due to the size and power of this bird only the most powerful clans could claim Thunderbird as their crest.

Hair Seal is the next figure on the Tanoo totem. Also known as the harbour seal, this is a species long favoured by zoos and sealand parks. It weighs up to 300 pounds and may attain a length of 70 inches, but the average size is much smaller than this. It lives off fish, octopus and shellfish, and prefers waters close to shore. There, in the shallows and rocks and reefs, the seal can escape its hungriest and fastest enemy, the killer whale. This defensive manoeuvre made the job of Haida hunters easier. Inshore, the seal could be hunted by men on foot. And seals were hunted year-round for their flesh and fat, the latter being one of the few local sources of fresh oil for the islanders during the winter months. Hunters probably also used the inflated skins as floats, just as the Nootka of Vancouver Island did on a larger scale when whaling.

Seal hunters are a common feature in Northwest Coast mythology, but Hair Seal—or Sea Lion which is remarkably similar in coastal art—is mentioned so seldom in Haida myth, it is conceivable that Seal is, like the Eagle, a late-comer to the hierarchy of crest and emblematic animals. Another example of this situation is that the wolf, common among the Tlingit, is not a crest animal in the islands, although they do make use of the Sea Wolf and the Sea Dog. In the case of the grizzly, also adopted from the Tlingit and Tsimshian, the Haida called him Grizzly Bear of the Sea.

Below Hair Seal on the totem is Sea Chief. He is one of the coast's mythical beings and one version of his story goes like this. Near Banks Island there dwelt a Saltwater or Sea Chief whose eyes dropped from their sockets each night and hung there, suspended, swinging in the moonlight. At meal times his family replaced his eyes in their sockets, otherwise he would not have been able to feed himself. What this chief liked best was hair seal, but as he had no teeth, he swallowed the meat in great chunks. Later he would burp and grunt and spit out the bones and gristle.

About all that is certain about this story is the location of Banks Island. Lying between Hecate Strait and Principe Channel, the island is in Tsimshian territory. The eyes dropping from their sockets—like water dripping rock to rock—probably refers to the tide dropping, and the toothless manner of eating is reminiscent of a blowhole in the rocks through which the rising tide roars and spits. The Gun is one such blowhole; to be found on North Beach near Masset, it is one of the best-known such holes on the coast.

Weeping Woman and Volcano Woman are other identities postulated for Sea Chief. No wonder Emily Carr called her painting of Sea Chief's face, "The Crying Totem". It is quite possible that her Haida guides thought this the proper name.

On Sea Chief's chest sits Frog. As there are no frogs on the Queen Charlotte Islands, this is either an imported crest or represents a toad; frequently the Haida considered them one and the same creature. Frog was the primary crest of Chief Edenshaw, a man who stands tall in Queen Charlotte Island history during the contact period. It is noteworthy that the death of Frog is the cause of the trouble in the Skidegate story of how Volcano Woman destroyed a village. Frog was also considered to be Thunderbird's watchman, so in this way it is related to two other figures on the Tanoo totem. Frogs were also carved on totems for it was believed that they would save the pole from burning or being cut down by strangers or those jealous of the family to whom the totem belonged.

If Frog is a toad he is the northwestern toad (*Bufo boreas boreas*) and is identifiable by his "warty skin, median greenish stripe, patotoid gland, and short hind legs with a brown spade on the foot." In size this toad varies in length from two to five inches and his colour varies from dark, or "reddish-brown background mottled with light brown, grey, or green."

The meaning or identity of the human figure seen grasping Killer Whale's tail below Frog is unknown. The killer whale (*Orcinus rectipinna*) is familiar in the waters off the Queen Charlotte Islands. It is a large porpoise-like whale with a prominent back fin and conspicuous white markings, with the males growing to a length of 26 feet and the females somewhat less. Like wolves they travel in packs— sometimes as many as a hundred can be seen together—and will eat almost anything they can catch, herring to whales.

The outreaching dorsal fin in this totem depiction is a fine realistic touch, for the tall dorsal is the killer whale's most distinctive feature, along with its black and white markings. The human figure does not imply that these whales will attack man, for they have never been known to do so. The figure may refer to a legend, a myth, an actual event, or again, it may represent a spirit caught in the act of transformation. Speculation aside, the immediate reason that Killer Whale is on this pole is because it was one of the crests belonging to the wife of the totem's owner.

The Sea Bear at the bottom of the pole is shown swallowing some sort of animal head first. Among the Haida the Sea Bear, as already stated, was sometimes their version of the mainland grizzly crest. What story this Sea Bear refers to is not known, but it is probably a reference to the Bear Mother story. In this ancient and widespread myth, a bear kidnaps a girl or woman picking berries and that winter she gives birth to twins. Some of the most dramatic and realistic argillite carvings depict elements of this story. The Bear, Grizzly, and Grizzly of the Sea were all important crests found on numerous Haida totems. A person using this crest was a member of the Raven clan.

THE WATCHMEN

Whenever possible the Haida built their villages facing south. As all but three or four of the winter villages of the Haida were on the eastern and northern coasts of the islands, this meant that the watchmen atop the totems were looking toward the mainland, Alaska or Vancouver Island. These were the cardinal points of every village's compass: people had always reached the Queen Charlotte Islands from these directions.

The Watchmen were looking the wrong way. Important visitors were on their way to the Queen Charlotte Islands. They were coming out of the southwest in a large vessel such as no Haida had ever seen. Those in their summer camps in the vicinity of Langara Island were the first people to see this vessel and they wasted no time in visiting the strangers.

CHAPTER THREE

WHERE HISTORY AND GEOGRAPHY COLLIDE

THE SPANISH ARRIVE

ON JULY 18, 1774, the first Europeans reached the Queen Charlotte Islands. The man given credit for this "discovery" was Juan Perez, commander of the *Santiago*. What the Haida thought when they went out and "discovered" the Europeans and their ship is unknown, but Perez's comments are known. He was not impressed by what he saw, noting only that land was sighted at 11 A.M. and there was nothing else new to report.

In a diary entry later that same day he observed that the distance between Puerto de Monterey and Punta de Santa Margarita was 423 leagues (1269 nautical miles). Today Perez's landmark is St. Margaret Point on Langara or North Island, the northernmost of the islands, and it is the oldest European place-name in British Columbia. Why Perez was so blase about this discovery is not known; that he was a good sailor but a particularly unimaginative man may be one reason; another reason Perez was not as excited by his find as he might have been can be attributed to his having sighted "signs of land" the day before.

What he had seen was bull kelp, which Perez described as looking like onions because of their large heads and long tails, adding that the Chinese call this kelp *"porras"*. Seeing the kelp was a happy event for Perez, who was now farther north than any Spaniard had previously sailed. As a seasoned pilot, Perez knew that this kelp was generally the first sign California-bound ships had that they were approaching

41

the coast. Notable, too, at this moment is his reference to China. This was the first recorded instance of China being mentioned on the Northwest Coast.

Late in the afternoon on the 19th, somewhere along the west coast of Langara Island, three canoes came out from the shore late in the afternoon. The men were good-looking with smiling faces and "beautiful eyes"; some of the men wore their hair tied back and their beards and mustaches reminded Perez of the Chinese he had encountered in Manila and other eastern ports. Judging from the location of the *Santiago*, these men were chiefs and shamans from one of the nearby summer camps, whose homes were likely the villages of either Dadens, Yaku or Kiusta.

Fray Juan Crespi, a priest from the Monterey mission, saw the visitors somewhat differently. "And we noticed," he wrote, "that a canoe came out from a break in the land like the mouth of a river [Parry Passage] and was paddled toward the ship. While it was still distant from the vessel we heard the people in it singing and by the intonation we know that they were pagans, for it was the same sung at the dances of pagans from San Diego to Monterey. They were eight men and a boy. Seven of them were paddling; the other, who was advanced in years, was upright and making dancing movements. Throwing several feathers into the sea, they made a turn about the ship."

He thought the men in the second canoe "corpulent and fat," but they had "good features with a red and white complexion and long hair. They were clothed in skins of the otter and the seawolf, as it seemed to us, and all, or most of them, wore well woven hats of rushes, the crown running up to a point. They are not noisy brawlers, all appearing to us to be of a mild and gentle disposition." [1]

From July 18 to 23, Perez remained in Dixon Entrance, during which time he sighted Cape Muzon and Forrester Island, two of Alaska's southeasternmost points. By July 23 the *Santiago* was west of Langara Island, back in the area where Perez made his first landfall. Now Perez was sailing south and making the biggest mistake of his career: he had not landed to make a formal claim to this new found land, contrary to his instructions, which ordered him to sail north to 60 degrees North Latitude and go ashore and claim the land for Spain. Perez had his reasons for not continuing northward. The weather was tetchy, the tidal currents powerful and unpredictable, the water supply was dangerously low and his men were beginning to show signs of scurvy. Besides, the *Santiago* was alone and hundreds of uncharted miles from home.

It was bad luck for Perez that he could not locate a safe anchorage that would enable him to go ashore. In July 1774 Perez's bad luck meant nothing more than cutting water rations; there would be other chances to go ashore, or so he thought. But in less than 20 years, in the courts of Spain and England, men would remember that Perez had not planted a cross and read the proclamation that would have made the land Spanish, a legal act recognized by every court in Europe. A few days later Perez made another attempt to find a harbour, this time at Barcaster Bay at the mouth of Nootka Sound on the outside coast of Vancouver Island, but the weather forced him off shore, where he decided to return to Monterey. This cost Spain dearly. Nearby, and only four years later, Captain James Cook went ashore on Bligh Island, thus establishing a British claim to the area.

Although it meant little to Juan Josef Perez Hernandez and his crew—many of whom were conscripted Indians and farmers from Mexico—they were the first Europeans known to have sighted the Queen Charlotte Islands. Despite the gallons of ink used by historians discussing Perez's failure to go ashore—undue caution being the favourite reason given by most critics—Perez proved that the North Pacific was not impenetrable. It is also true that Perez, in the 62-foot *Santiago*, with a sick crew and without the best of contemporary equipment and highly trained officers, saw more of the British Columbia coast than did Captain James Cook. Today his descriptions of the Haida, like those of Fray Crespi and his companion, Fray Tomas de la Pena, have great historical significance—and staying power; these diaries are abrim with colour, human interest, and the sort of details that are lacking in, say, the Russian accounts of 1741. This is equally true for most of the reports and descriptions left us by the first explorers and fur traders—frequently one and the same person.

OCEANIC ORIGIN THEORIES

However, Perez's logbooks and diaries were not published in full until the 20th century. Captain Cook did not see the Queen Charlotte Islands. A number of Spanish explorers were in the area in the late 18th century, but their reports and logbooks remained locked up in the Spanish archives for a hundred years. The first published reports of the Queen Charlotte Islands and the Haida reached Europe and North America through the books published by the American and British maritime fur traders who began reaching the islands as early as 1786. Although these books were followed by

Captain George Vancouver's justly famous *A Voyage of Discovery*, and a number of similar books, no one brought all the information together to create a picture of the Haida and their islands in the 18th century.

All the *Encyclopaedia Britannica* said about the islands in 1884 was that they were inhabited by the Haida, who lived on the coast of the islands and lived off fish they caught and potatoes that they grew. They tattooed themselves, sometimes painted their faces, and had some curious customs such as raising elaborately carved posts.

Many people reading this description could not help but be reminded of various South Pacific peoples who fished and carved poles and grew potatoes. Only 15 years after this *Britannica* entry was published, John Campbell, LL.D., sketched out his view of the South Pacific origin of the Haida. At a meeting of the Royal Society of Canada in 1897, Campbell presented a paper entitled "The Origin of the Haidahs of the Queen Charlotte Islands".

He opened his talk by observing: "While the society is celebrating the landfall of the illustrious John Cabot upon the eastern shore of our Dominion four hundred years ago, I have thought it not inappropriate to chronicle a possibly more ancient and more adventurous voyage that has left a permanent impression upon the islands of the far west. This voyage was undertaken at some remote period by the ancestors of those natives of the Queen Charlotte and adjoining islands now known as Haidahs."

"In their use of large canoes," Campbell said, picking up his original theme after a discussion of South Pacific peoples, "and in their proficiency in carving, as well as in the actual features of their idols and medicine posts, the Fijians claim kindred with the Haidahs, in spite of the difference in colour. The houses of the latter point to an insular origin as well as their maritime habits, but in the matter of dress, equipments, implements and folk-lore, it is hard to institute a comparison, partly for lack of material, partly because the Haidah has largely borrowed from his neighbour, the Tshimsiam."

Turning to linguistic similarities, he admitted that his evidence was lacking, but he was dead certain that, given time, he could prove the residents of the islands were Melanesian and Malayan. Continuing, Campbell pointed out that linguistic evidence proves that many groups of American people reached the Americas via the islands of the Pacific. After all, if early voyagers could reach Easter Island and the Hawaiian Islands, they might just as well have reached the Pacific Coast.

Campbell's argument is easy to follow. "The difficulty of a comparatively savage people traversing a wide ocean is an argument that should not weigh against the demonstration of language. The people of Easter Island came within eighteen hundred miles of the American coast, but, supposing them to have started from the Philippines, their route was one of eight thousand miles. Even recently, in comparatively small canoes, the islanders of the South Seas have made voyages of many hundreds of miles....The Haidahs, as a subordinate Melanesian people, probably found in rebellion against the Malay masters in some part of the archipelago, were, at some remote period, offered their choice between death and expatriation, and, spurned from every intermediate landing-place, at last found refuge on the uninhabited islands of the far east. This may have taken place at any time between the thirteenth and sixteenth centuries." [2]

Clearly, he wrote, the Haida must be late-comers—look where they live on the edge of the continent. Other American Indian tribes that he knew to have migrated from the South Pacific, such as the Algonquin people, were to be found in the Eastern Woodlands. Obviously, successive waves of later migrants from Japan and elsewhere had driven them east. These migrations or invasions began, Campbell thought, sometime about 800 A.D. in the Pacific Northwest. In all probability the Haida did not reach the coast until about 1500.

Asia

In 1898, Charles Hill-Tout, British Columbia's first amateur ethnologist, presented a paper noting his version of the origin of the west-coast people to the Royal Society of Canada. *The Salish People*, a four-volume work in which its editor has collected the best of Hill-Tout's work, is in print and is widely read; not so his 1898 presentation: "The Oceanic Origin of the Kwakiutl-Nootka and Salish Stocks of British Columbia and Fundamental Unity of Same with Additional Notes on the Dene." Another series of invasions was outlined in the 1980s by Ethel G. Stewart, a Canadian-American writer. Her *The Dene and Na-Dene Indian Migration 1233 A.D.* is subtitled *Escape from Genghis Khan*. The title may not be as misleading as the subtitle suggests. All of this might be irrelevant were it not for numerous remarks made by Marius Barbeau in various books he published in the 1940s and '50s. During his lifetime Barbeau was the world's leading authority on totem poles and argillite carvings. He repeatedly comments on Asian-Northwest Coast parallels. He claimed to have found echoes of Buddhist dirges in the songs on the Skeena River, and elsewhere seemed to think that the Dene people might be descendants of Mongolian soldiers who escaped eastward.

Right or wrong, Hill-Tout and Barbeau believed in what they had found and Barbeau, at least, had the evidence to support his statements. Although none of this relates directly to the Haida, it is well to remember how little is known of Haida language and prehistory.

No discussion of probable Asian contact along the Northwest Coast during its prehistory can ignore Thor Heyerdahl, the Norwegian anthropologist who, in the late 1940s, sailed a balsa raft named *Kon-Tiki* into history, film and literature. Unlike Campbell and Hill-Tout, Heyerdahl found it necessary to prove that ancient man could have reached the Americas by water; unlike them he did not see Polynesian immigrants populating the New World.

Heyerdahl's contention was much more complex. For him the origin of eastern Asiatic elements in Polynesia can be traced to the Hawaiian Islands. The only way this theory worked successfully for Heyerdahl was if he could prove that the Northwest Coast is seen as a second launching point; i.e. Asian sailors sailed first to the Northwest Coast and then set out for the Hawaiian Islands. Having lived in Bella Coola and Vancouver, he knew of the large coastal canoes that could make this coast a feasible, and, according to his theory, a logical and necessary jumping-off place.

In an interview in 1966 in Victoria, Heyerdahl suggested that the first large wave of migrants from Asia reached British Columbia's outermost islands about 200 BC. Other homeless travellers followed in later centuries, probably via coasting trips from China, Japan and Alaska. About 1100 AD a second wave of migration reached this coast, which is a much earlier date than those mentioned by Campbell, but it is not inconceivable that they are talking about either end of the same migration.

The story of history and geography colliding does not end here. Another chapter in the history of the Haida was first documented in Massachusetts, which was not inappropriate as most of the American maritime fur traders sailed out of Boston. There Horace Davis published his *Record of Japanese Vessels Driven Upon the Northwest Coast of America and Its Outlying Islands*. Not surprisingly, this small book is subtitled: *On the Likelihood of an Admixture of Japanese Blood on Our Northwest Coast*.

Davis' argument is not based on intermarriage as fact. It is his assumption that, since so many Japanese junks had been found adrift and derelict, or wrecked on shore throughout the Pacific, it stood to reason that junks now and again would have gone ashore more or less in one piece. Survivors of the long drift and subsequent shipwreck were, he thought a possibility. Why not? It had happened in 1833 near Cape Flattery.

Three crewmen survived the wreck of the *Hojun-maru* late in 1832 and its subsequent 14-month drift along the Japanese Current or Kuroshio. Rescued by the Makah people, the men were held as slaves until freed by Captain W.H. McNeill of the Hudson's Bay Company. Coincidentally, McNeill was the captain of the first HBC vessel to visit the islands and his wife was a Haida from Alaska. Their daughter married George Blenkinsop, an HBC employee, and went on to become one of Vancouver Island's founding matrons.

If no concrete evidence puts a junk ashore on the Queen Charlotte Islands, it is on record that in 1813 the brig *Forester* happened on a 700-ton derelict drifting 150 miles from the islands. Charles Brooks, in a book similar to Davis', published in San Francisco in 1876, states that a junk went ashore on the islands in 1831, but offers no further information.

Some ships, Japanese or otherwise, did go ashore. Almost 60 years earlier Juan Perez observed that the Haida who came out to trade with the officers and crew of the *Santiago* had iron objects "like half of a bayonet and a piece of a sword" lying in the bottoms of their canoes. Possibly these items were recovered from wrecks that drifted ashore. But if they did not come to the islands in Japanese junks, how did the iron reach the Haida?

ENGLAND AND SPAIN

There are a few obvious answers. Late in the 16th century both Sir Francis Drake and the mysterious Juan de Fuca, a ship's captain who seems to have spent most of his life in the employ of the Spanish navy in Mexico, sailed north of California to some unknown point. Little doubt exists in the minds of most authorities that these men were as far north as Vancouver Island, but how much farther north they went, and what they did, is open to conjecture. Since no official record of de Fuca's voyage is known to exist, his own account taken down in Venice in 1596 is all there is to go on. This would have been forgotten centuries ago were it not for two geographical details— Fuca's pillar and the Strait of Juan de Fuca, which are about where he said they were. There is no evidence as to Drake's whereabouts north of San Francisco Bay: the *Golden Hind's* logbook was given to Queen Elizabeth I on Drake's return to London and was not seen again.

Using information supplied by the Canadian novelist A.M. Stephen in his historical introduction to *The Kingdom of the Sun*, a novel set on the Northwest Coast, it is possible to speculate about another origin for the iron Perez recorded seeing in 1774.

"On the British Columbia Coast," he wrote, "there exists a tradition regarding the 'fair-haired' Haidas. It is said that, within the tribe, there existed until quite recently a number of natives whose hair was of a golden or reddish-brown colour." Having said this, Stephen made a leap of faith: "It seems highly improbable that the British Columbia Coast remained unvisited by Europeans previous to the voyages of Cook, Meares and Vancouver or to the recorded explorations of the later Spanish adventurers. It is possible that one or more of the Spanish galleons that never returned from Manila were swept north." [3]

Indian legend records one such galleon going ashore near Nehalem, a few miles south of the mouth of the Columbia River. This was probably the *San Francisco Xavier*, reported missing in 1707. At least one Haida legend gives credence to the notion that a galleon might have reached the Queen Charlottes. It is a complex and iconographic myth called The Shaman's Story involving a white man, a steel coat, smallpox, a ship and Moon's Daughter, among other things. This story was collected at Skidegate during the winter of 1900-01, and, while this proves nothing, the ethnologist who collected the story remarked on the American/British elements in the tale, and reported in a footnote that the Haida he talked to asserted this took place before any Europeans had visited the islands.

Bartholomew de Fonte may have been the white in a mail jacket that the Haida encountered, and whom their descendants forgot. His story, recorded in "A Letter from Admiral Bartholomew de Fonte, then Admiral of New Spain and Peru, and now Prince of Chili" appeared in a British magazine in 1708. Admiral de Fonte sailed into an incomprehensible landscape in 1640 and anchored before a place he called Mynhansset. Many since have thought this place might be Masset, among them the scientist George Mercer Dawson; others labelled the story nonsense.

About 1609 one Ferrer Maldonado, a Spaniard about whom more is known than either de Fonte or de Fuca, claimed to have sailed through the Strait of Anian or the Northwest Passage (from Davis Strait in the east to Bering Strait in the west) to the North Pacific in 1588. Nothing is known of his activities in the north and west. Maldonado claimed to have returned to the Atlantic Ocean and although geographers and historians have laughed at his story, the Arctic explorer Vilhjalmur Stefansson is on record as saying this voyage might have taken place, given near-perfect weather conditions.

In 1791, Don Juan Pantoja y Arriaga, the first explorer to sail into the unknown interior of the Strait of Juan de Fuca, met Indians in the vicinity of the San Juan Islands who told the Spaniards "there had been vessels within the canal much larger than [Arriaga's] schooner, one of which brought some bracelets of very fine brass engraved apparently with a burin, which they [the Indians] would not exchange [with Pantoja]." Henry R. Wagner, long the leading authority on Spanish exploration between Mexico and Vancouver Island, wrote in response to this statement: "This somewhat enigmatical sentence affords some proof that some one of the fur traders had reached the east end of the strait, or else the bracelets had come from some vessel in Queen Charlotte Sound."

Wagner has no explanation for what the Indians said next. "It was also learned from an Indian of eleven or twelve years of age, whom the storekeeper Jose Ignacio Gonzalez bought, that on the north side there is some flat country through which many people come to trade for fish and stay for two moons, bringing iron, copper, and blue beads, wearing distinct dress and having different bows and arrows, some larger than theirs, and with some large quadrupeds, with a round hoof, a mane, and a long tail." [4]

Bits of oral history such as this, and the remnants of Buddhist dirges found by Marius Barbeau on the Skeena River, are spots of light on an otherwise dark period of prehistory of the Northwest Coast.

GREECE AND ASIA

In the introduction to his novel, A.M. Stephen touched on another aspect of the ancient history of the Queen Charlotte Islands. "In appearance, the Haidas are distinctly superior to the Salish and the Kwakiutls who inhabit the adjacent shores, while their language differs radically from that of their neighbours. Their cosmogony links them with the Aztecs, the Mayas and Quiches of Central America and, consequently, with the Egyptian, Etruscan and Pelasgian Greek civilisations, which flourished in prehistoric ages beside the Mediterranean." [5]

Odd as this may sound, Perez described some of the Haida as being white and commented on their blue eyes. And a more recent reminder of this reputed past is to be found in Bill Reid and Robert Bringhurst's *The Raven Steals the Light*. "Haida Gwai, the Islands of the People, lie equidistant from Luxor, Machu Picchu, Nineveh and Timbuktu." [6]

An earlier piece of evidence supposedly confirming the link between the islands and the Far East was a bronze figurine dug up in a garden somewhere in the vicinity of Kincolith, a Nishga village near the mouth of the Nass River. Reportedly this discovery took place sometime around the turn of the century. This spot is about 100 miles northeast of Masset and a place to which the Haida went to fish eulachon every spring. In 1894 an expert in the Berlin museum compared this figurine to figures from Nepal and Calcutta and found it similar. "There is not the slightest embarrassment," added Professor O.T. Mason, an American authority, "in the way of this bronze image having been transported [via Spanish vessels crossing the Pacific Ocean between Mexico and the Malay Archipelago] from Manila to British Columbia at any time between 1570 and 1770." [7]

More tenuous, but no less interesting, is a comment made by Nigel Davies in his *Voyagers to the New World*. "The 'split-image' comprises a drawing in which an animal illustration is cut in two from head to tail; the two halves are then pulled apart and laid out on a flat surface facing each other, with the twin profiles joined together only at mouth and nose. This strange motif was used in archaic China in 1200 B.C. but survived into recent times among the Haida." [8]

The Orient and British Columbia. Perez, as a pilot on the galleon route between California and Manila, knew the Chinese so well he recognized bull kelp by its Chinese name—*porras*—and one of the first things he said about the Haida was that they wore their hair tied back like the Chinese, and their beards and mustaches reminded him of the Orient.

Perez's observations are not surprising. By about 1000 A.D. the Chinese had established trade with the Arab world and within another 400 years Chinese fleets had explored the Indian Ocean, an area the Portuguese began exploring late in the 15th century. Arabs were the main traders in the Indian Ocean at that time. In 1571—50 years after Magellan discovered the Philippines—Manila became Spain's administrative centre in Southeast Asia. In the same year Canton became the official Chinese-Portuguese trading centre. Perez had possibly spent time in Canton, no one knows for sure, but as a pilot on the Manila galleons there can be no doubt about his knowing Manila, where Chinese traders were commonplace.

Picking up another Chinese-Northwest Coast story by one of its loose ends, it is important to know that the Chinese had established themselves in the area of modern Afghanistan by 126 BC. There the Chinese would have met Greek traders, who had known the area for centuries, and later the Chinese came into contact with the Roman Empire. The known world grows smaller. Trade routes made travel relatively easy, so it is not surprising to find a Buddhist monk of Afghan birth in China about 450 AD.

Hwui Shan was the monk's name. Sometime around 460, in company with other holy men, Hwui visited Hokkaido, Japan's northernmost island. From there the men sailed along the Kuril Islands to Kamchatka, which had been known to the Chinese for 700 years. From here on Hwui Shan's geography lacks details; still, it seems he visited the Aleutian Islands and the coasts of Alaska and British Columbia, wherever else he may have gone.

One detail in this account may anchor part of Hwui Shan's story in British Columbia. "They make a ditch which is filled with water-silver," he wrote, "and the rain flows over the water-silver." Generations of historians have discounted this brief but poetic description, thinking it a meaningless detail; others have seen the "water-silver" as ice. Bruce McKelvie, long one of British Columbia's most popular and inquisitive historians, saw something else. For him, the ditches were pits dug by the coastal Indians to fill with eulachon, one of the major sources of grease for the Haida and Tsimshian. As the fish rotted, the precious oil rose to the surface of the water, bringing with it fish scales glittering "water-silver". [9]

The Chinese connection grows stronger as stories emerge from other far-flung corners of British Columbia. During the 1860s miners in the Cassiar district, a gold-rush area deep in the Coast Mountains, found a cache of 3,000-year-old Chinese coins. A hundred years later on Saturna Island, between Vancouver and Victoria, a shard was found, which officials of the Royal British Columbia Museum identified as Oriental and dated to 300 AD. Anchors of a type used by Chinese mariners were recently discovered off the coast of California and in British Columbia a Chinese urn, possibly 300 years old, was discovered in a wreck near Bamfield on the west coast of Vancouver Island.

That nothing Chinese has turned up in the Queen Charlotte Islands is no indication that Chinese voyagers were not there or did not know of the place. What could or would have survived? Nothing exists today from the voyages of Perez, Cook and the early maritime fur traders. Nor is it surprising that no official records of these voyages exist in China. For one thing, Chinese history is to some extent a mystery. It would be little short of a miracle had original documents survived into modern times. Like our own histories,

Chinese histories are based on what has survived—the records past generations have thought worth keeping.

And if records are the final word, what about the lack of prehistoric arrowheads in the islands? None have yet been discovered by archeologists, but the same men do not doubt their existence. Yet these scientists shrug off the similarities between Haida and South Pacific fish hooks and maintain that the almost identical appearance of Haida and New Zealand houseposts and totem poles is coincidental. Like most people, scientists see what they want to.

Recently, archeologists have begun to think about prehistoric migrations from the Aleutians and northern Alaska along the coast to British Columbia. However, Marius Barbeau suggested in the mid-1940s that the Haida were possibly migrants who had worked their way south along the coast until they reached the Queen Charlottes. No one paid any attention.

The more probing that is done, the less coincidental it seems that Hwui Shan reached North America via Japan, Kamchatka and the Aleutians; these places form the shoreline of the Japanese current and its eddies. When did the first Chinese or Japanese sailor discover this current? Some wrecked Japanese sailors were certainly able to repair their ships and return home. After a winter on Bering Island in eastern Siberia in 1741-42, the survivors of the crew of the *St. Peter* rebuilt their ship from the wreckage and sailed back to Petropavlovsk that same summer. Nothing is impossible; deeds can be forgotten due to bad management of records or a breakdown in the oral tradition. It is known that the Polynesians had explored and colonized their Pacific world by 800 AD, yet their descendants had forgotten the voyages by the 16th century, when the Europeans made their first forays into the area.

Western scholars long doubted the voyage of Semen Dezhnev, but records recently published prove he discovered and sailed through the Bering Strait in 1648. These records had been misplaced, so when Vitus Bering, knowing nothing of the earlier voyage, rediscovered the strait in 1728, he named it in his own honour. Other similar instances abound in the annals of Atlantic and Pacific exploration, so it is not inconceivable that travel routes in the North Pacific may be older, and may have once been far better known, than is suspected today.

JUMPING OFF TO THE HAWAIIAN ISLANDS

Although he may never have seen a Haida canoe, John Campbell understood what their size meant. In his paper to the Royal Society of Canada, he observed: "The Haidahs appear to have kept up their love of large canoes. The dug-out which carried Mr. Poole from the Queen Charlotte islands to the mainland had three jury-rigged masts and a main stay-sail, and carried thirty-seven people with two tons of freight. From whatever point the ancestors of the Haidahs set out on the voyage that landed them in their American home, that voyage must have been a long and distressing one, yet not an impossibility to people inured to a rough life on the sea." [10]

"Mr. Poole" was the already mentioned Francis Poole, the first white resident of the Queen Charlotte Islands, where he went in search of copper for the QCI Mining Company. This was in 1862 and his base was Burnaby Island off the southeast coast of Moresby Island. His *Queen Charlotte Islands, A Narrative of Discovery and Adventure in the North Pacific*, published in 1872 was, for Americans and Europeans alike, the first popular account of life in the islands.

The canoe mentioned by Campbell belonged to Chief Klue or Kloo, of Tanu, a town of about 600 inhabitants on Tanu Island, about midway down the east coast of Moresby Island. The first glimpse Poole gives us of the canoe, is at about noon when the "grand state-canoe, which my men had never seen and did not know of came paddling and sailing like a huge swan round the headland."

Village of Tanu in 1878. (COURTESY GEOLOGICAL SURVEY OF CANADA)

There were actually two canoes and Poole's "company consisted of two distinct parties....The first was made up of one of the Skid-a-gate chiefs and six of his tribe, three males and three females. They were in a cedar canoe, fourteen feet in length. It carried those seven persons, with their goods, weighing about half a ton, well; but it appeared a mere cock-boat in face of yon out-spanning ocean."

In the second canoe there were "Chief Klue, five young Klootchmen [women], and thirty men, together with myself....Besides our personal weight, we had shipped two tons of freight, namely, a bundle for each Indian, my goods and chattels, and the rest in copper or other ores. Our canoe was what is known in the Far West as a dug-out. Klue had cut and constructed it, foot by foot, with his own hands, out of cedar-wood (thuja gigantea) [*Thuja plicata* or Western red cedar]. It carried three jury-masts and a considerable show of canvas, not to mention a main staysail. A proud and truly inspiring sight was it to view all this canvas spread out to the breeze and to see thirty-seven human beings all paddling together, with regularity, precision, and force." In all fairness, however, if the transpacific theories are to be understood in their entirety, there was more to Poole's trip—and hundreds of similar trips—than the beauty of the Haida canoe.

From Tanu, Klue and his men hugged the shore south to Cape St. James and there they camped for the night. The next morning they planned to cross Queen Charlotte Sound to the east coast of Vancouver Island. But when they awoke the weather looked as though it was turning bad, so the Haida decided to stay put, at which point Poole made an observation that Campbell neglected to quote. "The Klue Indians are reputed to be the most venturesome of all canoemen in the North Pacific, and I do not wish to defame them, but the contrary. Still, it [their travel] is always within sight of land. At the thought of trusting themselves to the high seas they quail. On this occasion they would have shirked it altogether, only for their confidence in my guidance."

Like the Greek sailors, the Haida were a coasting people, going ashore nightly to camp or wait out inclement weather. On this trip Poole and his Haida canoemen waited for thee days for the weather to clear and then set sail again only to be hit by a sudden storm that seemed to go with them no matter how hard they paddled. After almost 24 hours of non-stop work, dawn found them approaching Banks Island, directly east of Skidegate; even while paddling they had been going backwards. At some point during the storm the canoe with the Skidegate chiefs disappeared and did not reappear for several days, having been driven north to Fort Simpson, near present-day Prince Rupert.

Twenty-two days later Poole reached Victoria. His trip was "undoubtingly acknowledged to be the greatest canoe voyage ever known in the North Pacific, and that too along a coast full of dangers...and at a season of the year when all British Columbian vessels give the land a wide berth." [11]

The story of the beautiful Haida canoe, just like the story of Poole's trip, has two perspectives. One school of thought considers the Haida great seamen and travellers, and the other does not. The first school believes that the size of the Haida canoe, plus the location of the Queen Charlotte Islands, which made canoe travel an inescapable element of Haida life, would allow the Haida to go where they wished. The second school maintains that until the late 18th century the Haida did not have sails, which would have limited sea travel. Not until the missionaries taught the Haida how to put ribs in their canoes would they stand up to bad weather. Had the Haida been more at home at sea, so this argument goes, instead of waiting for dead whales to wash ashore they would have gone whaling as did the Nootka of Vancouver Island and the Olympic Peninsula. What both schools do agree upon is that the Haida canoe, as known since the 1860s, is a work of art. Whether this was always the case is another matter. Perez was impressed by the size of the canoes he observed, and so were many other traders and explorers, but few speak of the beauty of these dugouts.

It was 125 years after Perez's arrival that a mariner was impressed sufficiently by the potential of these canoes to put the possibilities to use. In 1901, Captain John Claus Voss bought a 38-footer, decked her over, added a cabin, ribs and a keel, and, after naming her *Tilikum* ("friend" in Chinook, the coastal trading jargon), sailed her from Victoria to Australia, and then on to Cape Town. From there Voss, who is considered by many to have been the finest small-craft sailor of the first half of the 20th century, sailed her to South America, on to the Azores, and up the Thames to London.

It is not known if this canoe was of Haida manufacture, but it is safe to presume so; Haida canoes were legendary and it does not stand to reason that Voss would have settled for second best. According to one of the men who sailed aboard her, the *Tilikum* was a 100-year-old war canoe, which Voss bought for 80 silver dollars. After Voss purchased her and moved her to Oak Bay near Victoria, she was completely rebuilt for her epic voyage, so the *Tilikum* was hardly an Indian canoe when she sailed into the Pacific. The first unmodified canoe to follow in the *Tilikum's* wake was the *Orenda*, a 42-foot canoe built to 19th-century specifications and sailed by three whites. She made it to Hawaii, her destination.

If Heyerdahl's theories are correct, the *Orenda* followed the exact path of her ancestors when Eastern Asiatic peoples on the Pacific Coast migrated into the Pacific. Old legends claim the Hawaiian Islanders once built their huts facing east, the direction whence their ancestors had come. In that land from which those people had sailed, it was said, the trees shed their leaves once a year. More than one person has suggested these trees were on the Queen Charlotte Islands.

A report published by the Canadian geologist George Dawson contains supporting information. In 1885 he had visited the northern end of Vancouver Island and talked to the Kwakiutl about their language, legends and customs. As well, he talked to the missionaries living among them. There, Dawson learned the stories concerning Kan-e-a-ke-luh, a cultural hero of sorts who created life as it is still known among the Kwakiutl of the Cape Scott-Beaver Cove area, about 140 miles from the Queen Charlotte Islands.

Where this hero came from or where he went is unknown. Heyerdahl refers to him as Kane, identifying him as the wanderer figure. The Maori of New Zealand called a similar character Tane. Readers of Pacific Coast Indian mythologies will recognize Raven and Mink as less sophisticated versions of Kane. When he left this coast the wanderer went "very far away and disappearing altogether from mortal ken, so that the people supposed the sun to represent him". In other words, he went toward the setting sun. Of Kan-e-a-ke-luh, in a footnote to his report, Dawson wrote: "One cannot but be struck, however, with the close resemblance of this word to kanaka, the Hawaiian word for 'man.' Is it within the bounds of possibility, that the story of the arrival of this culture-hero depends on some historical event perhaps connected with the period of remarkable movement and adventurous sea voyages which [Abraham] Fornander shews [in his *An Account of the Polynesian Race*] to have occurred in the Polynesian region, about the eleventh or twelfth centuries of our era?" [12]

Such trips would require canoes and while the Haida canoe—or any Northwest Coast canoe for that matter—may have been capable of reaching the Hawaiian Islands, there is reason for lingering doubt. Chief Weah of Masset is quoted as having told one ethnologist some years ago that the Haida did not build sea-going canoes before 1640. How he knew the exact date is not explained, but—remembering John Campbell's estimate that the Haida did not reach the islands before 1500—something may have happened about five centuries ago, something that lived on in the memories of the chiefs. Maybe it got twisted around in the telling; maybe the Haida *stopped* making sea-going voyages sometime around 500 years ago.

Admittedly, a Haida canoe prior to European modifications may have been a frail vessel, but it was as large as, or at least comparable in size to many of the Spanish vessels. The *Santiago* may have been as much as 80 feet long at waterline or as little as 62, historians do not agree, and the *Sonora*, which Bodega y Quadra sailed to Alaska in 1775, was several feet short of 40. The *St. Peter* and *St. Paul* of Vitus Bering's second expedition in 1741 from Kamchatka through the Aleutian Islands to Southeast Alaska, which at any time of the year is one of the world's worst seaways, were 80-footers—and their planks were lashed to the ships' frames. Voss sailed with one companion; Quadra with two officers and ten sailors. Aboard the *Sonora* there was no room to walk, no room to stretch out to sleep. Further: she was built for coasting voyages between San Blas and Baja California. A fleet of sea-going canoes, such as those described as being used by Polynesian travellers, were cleaner, more comfortable, faster and easier to sail, and, as the voyages proved, more seaworthy.

When the first British and American explorers reached the Hawaiian Islands, the people were using logs that had drifted in from the Northwest Coast to make their sea-going canoes. In story after story the Haida-Hawaiian connections are outlined, from the similarities between the two peoples to the way they built boats and houses and how they carved and worshipped. Whatever else one may add to this, and Heyerdahl in one book uses 78 pages to document the Northwest Coast-Polynesia connection, one thing remains constant. To paraphrase Heyerdahl: the Haida, born on the edge of a continent, and living their lives out at the jumping-off spot to the Pacific heartland, were as close to Hawaii as Hawaiians were to Tahiti and Samoa.

PARADOX

A good deal of Haida history is hinted at in the interviews done by Barbeau in the 1930s. Mention is made of voyages and events that can never be proven. There are also stories that were still traditional well into the 20th century that tell of people who would become

Haida moving up the coast from Puget Sound. Such hints bring to mind an intriguing story collected by Swanton, which says that the Haida—at least the people who would call themselves Haida—were not alone on their islands even in recent times. A village known as Songs of Victory Town was located near Roe Point between Hewlett Bay and Douglas Inlet at the northwestern corner of Moresby Island. The people living there were known as the Pitch People and they controlled the local coast between the village of Kaisun and Tasu Sound. They were driven out of this area by the Sea Lion Town People and moved to the outside coast. "They were always looked upon as an uncultivated branch of Haida, and are said not to have possessed any crests." Survivors later intermarried with the Cumshewa people, some of whom as late as 1901 claimed descent from them, but none of the Pitch People survived.

Only a few things are known about these people. Kaisun belonged to them and they are sometimes described as Ravens, and they were either driven off or died off, and their town was taken over by the Sea Lion Town People, who were Eagles. The Pitch People were big and strong and—judging from the stories—not very smart. This is a very European note: since the dawn of time Europeans have thought strangers barbaric and stupid. Most of the Haida accounts of these people claim they had no crests and fished in the dark, because "the black cod came to the surface of the sea during the night." [13]

Racial jokes from the edge of history! At first glance these stories tell of a people, possibly a Raven group, supplanted by the growing power of Eagles and other clans moving onto the islands from the Aleutians and the northern coast. It is entirely plausible that the Pitch People were the original Ravens, a people who had settled on the islands centuries earlier; perhaps the language called Haida was theirs. This implies that the people Perez and other early visitors knew as Haida were late-comers who were still adapting themselves to a Northwest Coast maritime culture, and adds yet another dimension to the mystery of the Queen Charlotte Islands.

This history is doubtless too much of a patchwork ever to be pieced together satisfactorily. Each element is an episode and like the figures on the totems can be interpreted in various ways—as history, symbols, family trees and crests—and no interpreter can ever be sure of being quite right. Another factor is that, like so much else on the Queen Charlotte Islands, many of these episodes are paradoxical. On one hand the Haida may be superior to other peoples on the Northwest Coast; on the other the Haida may be inferior because the islands attracted fugitives and travellers from up and down the coast. In this scenario the islands were the great coastal melting pot.

Another paradox is compounded by a certain amount of irony. Various Anglophiliac writers have attributed the discovery of the islands to Captain Cook. Others, ignoring Perez and the islands, have Cook discovering the British Columbia coast at Nootka Sound. The truth of the matter is: Perez discovered the islands, but it was Cook's discovery of Nootka Sound that led to the exploration and exploitation of the Queen Charlotte Islands.

CHAPTER FOUR

THESE FORTUNATE ISLANDS

CAPTAIN JAMES COOK and his men spent 31 days at Nootka Sound on the west coast of Vancouver Island during March and April of 1778. Most of this time was spent surveying the area, repairing the *Discovery* and *Resolution*, and brewing spruce beer, which was, after almost two years at sea, the only specific available to Cook in his constant fight against scurvy. The men mixed freely with the local West-Coast People and did a good deal of trading. Among the items the crews received in their bartering were sea otter pelts.

Months later at Kamchatka, a merchant willingly paid Cook's men 30 rubles per sea otter pelt. A year later at Canton one sailor sold his entire collection of skins for $800; others sold prime pelts for $120 apiece. At this point the crews almost mutinied when their demands to return to the Northwest Coast to buy more furs and make their fortunes were not met. When Cook's *A Voyage to the Pacific Ocean* was published in 1784 the world learned of the trading potential Cook's men had discovered. To make trading easier, Cook had drawn up a virtual blueprint to guide future traders. A year later the first fur trader sailed for the Northwest Coast.

NAMES AND SHADOWS

The *Harmon*, commanded by James Hanna, spent the season of 1785 at Nootka Sound. A year later Hanna returned, this time in command of the *Sea Otter*, but another ship had already bought up the available furs, so Hanna sailed north up the west coast of

Vancouver Island. During this leg of his trip, he supposedly saw land to the north, which he named Nova Hibernia. What he saw may have been the Queen Charlotte Islands, but he did not reach the islands, as is sometimes claimed.

The British captains Henry Laurie and John Guise, in the *Captain Cook* and *Experiment*, may have traded along the east coast of the islands in 1786 but if so, they left no trace. The names of the first maritime fur traders known to have reached the islands were recorded in a log three years afterward.

This log was kept by Robert Haswell, second officer on the *Columbia*. The ship reached Houston Stewart Channel, the channel separating Moresby and Kunghit islands, in June 1789 and, Haswell wrote, no time was wasted. "A brisk trade was soon set on foot by Coya the Chief who bartered for all his Subjects, and a number of Sea Otter skins were purchaced before night. Iron was of far less value with them than with those natives we were last with cloathing was most in demand these people had been visated by several navigaters they spoke distinctly of Colinnet and Dunkin and they brought a pece of Paper that Informed us the NW American Schooner had been here May the 24th last." [1]

"Colinnet and Dunkin" were James Colnett and Charles Duncan, captains of the *Prince of Wales* and *Princess Royal*, respectively. Charles Duncan is a mysterious figure, who enters history as an experienced naval officer in 1786 and disappears from the record in 1792. James Colnett's story is quite different. A great deal is known about his 35 years at sea: how he started out as an able seaman and then served as a midshipman under Captain James Cook during the latter's second voyage into the Pacific, and how he got mixed up with John Meares—the congenital liar whose stories about his activities at Nootka Sound brought Britain and Spain to the brink of war in 1790. This association with Meares led to Colnett's arrest by the Spanish authorities at Nootka Sound in July 1789. After leaving the Northwest Coast, Colnett returned to active duty in the Royal Navy and became a surveyor of some distinction.

The *North West America*, built at Nootka Sound in 1788 by John Meares' Chinese carpenters, and the first ship built on the Northwest Coast, was commanded by one Robert Duffin. He apparently traded briefly with the Haida in May 1788. Later, on Meares' orders, Duffin supposedly sailed into the Strait of Juan de Fuca in 1788 and claimed the area for the British. He was still on the coast in 1792 and is mentioned in the logs of Captain George Vancouver.

Between the visits of Colnett, Duffin and Duncan in the mid-1780s and June 1799, when Richard Jeffry Cleveland, master of the *Caroline*, traded along the east coast, more than 50 ships are known to have visited the islands. Surprisingly, considering the amount written about this period, very little is known of the activities of most of these visitors and next to nothing about the Haida at this time. Some of the ships' records are not known to exist, others are vague. This silence underlines once again the importance of the few days Juan Perez and his men spent in the vicinity of Langara Island. The information found in Juan Perez's papers, in the diaries kept by the two priests who were aboard the *Santiago*, provides the first clear picture of the Haida at the instant of contact.

BLUE EYES

The Haida were lucky that their first encounter was with Juan Perez. He was an explorer, and was under the strictest orders when he set out from San Blas, Mexico, not to disturb the people he might meet. If he found native settlements wherever he might go ashore, he must deal with them "affectionately", commanded Viceroy Antonio Maria Bucareli y Ursua in his instructions. Perez must give them the trade goods that he had been provided with for that purpose. And then, to the best of his ability, he was to learn whatever he could about these peoples and their cultures, their geography and politics, religion and history.

More important than any of this, Perez must learn from these Indians whether other whites had established contact with them and what their aims and ambitions were; all of this Perez was to learn in detail, no matter the difficulty, and if necessary by sign language.

Also, Perez was not to "take anything from the Indians against their will, but only in barter or given by them through friendship. All must be treated with kindness and gentleness, which is the most efficacious means of gaining and firmly establishing their esteem. Thus, those who may return to these places for the purpose of establishing settlements, if it be so decided, will be well received." [2]

Four journals were kept by men aboard the *Santiago*, and the initial encounter with the Haida is recorded almost brilliantly, considering the silence of the first British fur traders.

Just after dawn, wrote Fray Tomas de la Pena, "the wind came from east-southeast...the fog continued very dense and wet. About nine o'clock the course was altered...[so] that we might examine the low land that showed at the end of the point....it consisted of three small islands which were near the mainland. These the Captain named the Islands of Santa Margarita, this being the day of that glorious lady. It was impossible to get an observation today on account of the heavy fog and drizzle....[that afternoon] we saw bonfires on the land, and presently there came to us a canoe with nine men in it. This canoe drew near to the vessel, the pagans in it singing; but they would not come near enough for us to communicate by means of signs."

About five that afternoon the same canoe returned, along with another. Perez gave the men beads and in return the Haida gave the Spaniard dried fish. "These persons are well-built," the priest wrote, "white, with long hair; and they were clothed in pelts and skins, some of them were bearded. They had some iron implements in their canoes, but we were unable to inquire where they obtained them, for presently they went back to land, inviting us thither, and offering to give us water on the following day."

The next afternoon 21 canoes visited the *Santiago*. Fray Pena noted that most of the canoes were filled with men, but the arrival of one that was not was the starting point for one of the best descriptions to come from the Perez expedition.

The canoe that held the good father's attention was full of women. "At the time the women's canoe arrived at the ship it happened that its prow struck that of another canoe whose occupants were men and broke it; at this the men became very angry, and one of them, seizing the prow of the women's canoe, broke it to pieces in order to repay their carelessness. All the afternoon these canoes, twenty-one in all, were about the ship, their occupants trading with the ship's people, for which purpose they had brought a great quantity of mats, skins of various kinds of animals and fish, hats made of rushes and caps made of skins, bunches of feathers arranged in various shapes, and, above all, many coverlets, or pieces of woven woolen stuffs very elaborately embroidered and about a yard and a half square, with a fringe of the same wool about the edges and various figures embroidered in different colours.

"Our people bought several of all these articles, in return for clothing, knives and beads. It was apparent that what they like most were things made of iron; but they wanted large pieces with a cutting edge, such as swords, wood-knives and the like—for, on being shown ribands they intimated that these were of trifling value, and, when offered barrel hoops, they signified that these had no edge. Two of the pagans came aboard the ship, and were much pleased with the vessel and things on board of it.

"The women have the lower lip pierced, and pendent therefrom a flat round disk [labret]; we were unable to learn the significance of this, nor of what material the disk was made. Their dress consists of a cape with a fringe about the edge and a cloth reaching to the feet, made of their woven woolen stuff, or of skins, and covering the whole body. Their hair is long and falls in braids to the shoulder. They are as fair and rosy as any Spanish woman, but are rendered ugly by the disk they have in the lip, which hangs to the chin. The men also are covered, with the skins or with the woven cloths of wool, and many have capes like those of the women; but they do not hesitate about remaining naked when occasion for selling their clothing offers.

"At six o'clock, taking leave of us, they made for the land, and they made evident their desire that we should go thither. Some sailors went down into the canoes and the pagans painted their faces with delight and shouts of joy. These pagans gave us to understand that we should not pass on to the northward because the people there were bad and shot arrows and killed. How common it is for pagans to say that all are bad except themselves!" [3]

How little attention has been paid to Fray Pena's observations that long-ago July afternoon is attested to in one prominent scholar's claim that it is silly to believe that the Haida had woollen cloth; nor could they have tools and weapons of metal. Furthermore: the men were not white and the women were certainly not good-looking. This dates from the 1960s; happily, the priest was not the only person aboard the *Santiago* to report what he saw.

A recently translated letter from Juan Perez to Viceroy Bucareli, dated August 31, 1774, clearly states that he encountered 200 or more Indians—men, women and children, who came out to meet the *Santiago* in 21 canoes—at 55 degrees North Latitude. "They were a beautiful people indeed, the men and women alike, being white complexioned, [with] fair hair and eyes blue and brown. They were very docile, judging by the appearance of those who came along side."

There were no further encounters with the Haida. Generally the weather was squally, when not wet and foggy: in other words, typical weather for the northwest coast of the islands. But there were those moments that linger in memory. On the afternoon of July 24 "the wind died away...to a dead calm during the night. At sundown land was seen, and it seemed to us to be that which we saw first as we approached the coast on the eighteenth instant. At eleven at night there was an appearance in the sky, in the north and the northeast, of some very brilliant northern lights." [4]

That was that. A year later Perez would sail north again, once again on the *Santiago*, but this time as second officer under Bruno de Hezeta (sometimes spelled Heceta). The *Santiago* reached the west coast of Vancouver Island at which point Hezeta, possibly because of Perez's dire warnings, turned homeward. The expedition's second vessel, the tiny *Sonora*, a 36-foot schooner captained by Juan Francisco de la Bodega y Quadra, sailed past the Queen Charlotte Islands and on to Bucareli Bay near the present location of the village of Craig in Southeastern Alaska. On his return he named the large body of water, which Perez had thought the mouth of a great enclosure, Entrada de Perez, but the name would not stick. It is now Dixon Entrance.

THE FRENCH ARRIVE

Not even an echo of this encounter with Perez and the *Santiago* has survived in the oral history of the Haida. Nor does tradition have anything to say about another visitor: the French explorer Jean Francois de Galaup, Comte de La Perouse, commanding the *Astrolabe* and *Boussole*, who arrived in 1786. He was on a world cruise, one that he and his ships would not survive, but his reputation has survived: many think him second only to Captain James Cook as a Pacific explorer. He had been ordered to the Northwest Coast to look at that part of the coast Cook had ignored. This was a lot of country. Cook had not seen anything but glimpses of the coast of Washington and had missed most of Vancouver Island, the Queen Charlottes and Prince of Wales Island in Alaska. On the Northwest Coast his reputation rests on the time he spent at Nootka Sound. So far as the British Columbia coast is concerned, La Perouse did not fill in many blanks left by Cook—except in the Queen Charlotte Islands.

On August 19, coasting south from Alaska, he sighted and named the Kerouart Islands. A nearby point was called Point Hector, but would soon be renamed Cape St. James. Sailing east, La Perouse rediscovered Entrada de Perez—and ran head on into the same current ("the waters within it flowing with more violence than even in a narrower strait") that had driven Perez back from a hoped-for anchorage in 1774. Turning back without having seen signs of the Haida, La Perouse continued on to Nootka Sound, where he reported on the Russian activities in Alaska to Estevan Martinez, who was now in command of the Spanish forces in the North Pacific. The

Northwest Coast was rapidly becoming an extension of Europe with all of its old-country alliances and prejudices.

So far as our knowledge of the Haida is concerned, after Perez's departure in 1774 the Queen Charlotte Islands simply disappeared from view until the arrival of Captain George Dixon, commanding the *Queen Charlotte*, in July 1787.

VOYAGE OF THE *QUEEN CHARLOTTE*

Providentially for future readers, Captain George Dixon's time in the islands was well-documented in *A Voyage Around the World*, published shortly after Dixon's return to England. Although not the first account of trading with the Haida, it remains the best and happiest.

Aboard Captain Dixon's ship, the supercargo or official trader was William Beresford, and it was he who wrote the bulk of *A Voyage Around the World* in the form of letters home. Dixon added front and back matter and put his own name on the title page. This is the first book in English to offer a picture of the islands, which partially explains why some historians gave Dixon credit for discovering the islands. The rest of the explanation is due to silence: Perez's account, along with those of the two priests aboard the *Santiago*, was virtually unknown to the English-speaking world until late in the 19th century.

Dixon had served under Captain Cook, as had Colnett, and was with Cook at Nootka Sound and knew first-hand how eager the Indians were to trade sea otter skins and other peltries for iron. And he knew from personal experience what Russian and Chinese merchants would pay for these furs so easily and cheaply obtained from the Indians of the Northwest Coast.

Early in 1785 London businessmen put together a company known to history as the King George's Sound Company. It was this company that sent Dixon to the Northwest Coast in the *Queen Charlotte*, but the leader of the expedition was Nathaniel Portlock, captain of the *King George*. The two ships sailed from England late in August 1785 and reached Alaska's Cook Inlet the following July. They wintered in the Hawaiian Islands and returned to Alaska in the spring of 1787, and, after assisting John Meares, who had wintered in Prince William Sound, Dixon and Portlock parted company in their search for untouched trading areas. Dixon sailed south and, in a manner of speaking, rediscovered the Haida and their island world. That he was a good man, as well as an experienced trader, may account for Dixon's success and pleasant days among the Haida.

Late in June the *Queen Charlotte* sighted the islands and a few days later, sailing south down the west coast, "The Indians we fell in with in the morning of the 2d of July, did not seem inclined to dispose of their cloaks, though we endeavoured to tempt them by exhibiting various articles of trade, such as toes [chisels or spikes], hatchets, adzes, howels [cooper's planes], tin kettles, pans, &c. their attention seemed entirely taken up with viewing the vessel, which they apparently did with marks of wonder and surprise. This we looked on as a good omen, and the event showed, that for once we were not mistaken.

"After their curiosity, in some measure, subsided, they began to trade, and we presently bought what cloaks and skins they had got, in exchange for toes, which they seemed to like very much.

"By ten o'clock we were within a mile of the shore, and saw the village where these Indians dwelt right abreast of us: it consisted of about six huts, which appeared to be built in a more regular form than any we had yet seen, and the situation very pleasant....A scene now commenced, which absolutely beggars all description, and with which we were so overjoyed, that we could scarcely believe the evidence of our senses. There were ten canoes about the ship, which contained, as nearly as I could estimate, 120 people; many of these brought most beautiful beaver [sea otter] cloaks; others excellent skins, and, in short, none came empty handed, and the rapidity with which they sold them, was a circumstance additionally pleasing; they fairly quarrelled with each other about which should sell his cloak first; and some actually threw their furs on board, if nobody was at hand to receive them; but we took particular care to let none go from the vessel unpaid.

"Toes were almost the only article we bartered with on this occasion, and indeed they were taken so very eagerly, that there was not the least occasion to offer anything else. In less than half an hour we purchased near 300 beaver skins, of an excellent quality; a circumstance which greatly raised our spirits, and the more, as both the plenty of fine furs, and the avidity of the natives in parting with them, were convincing proofs, that no traffic whatever had recently been carried on near this place, and consequently we might expect a continuation of this plentiful commerce....[So that you may] form some idea of the cloaks we purchased here, I shall just observe, that they generally contain three good sea otter skins, one of which is cut in two pieces, afterwards they are neatly sewed together, so as to form a square, and are loosely tied about the shoulders with small leather strings fastened on each side."

The next day the only Indians to visit the *Queen Charlotte* were those who had traded so enthusiastically on July 2nd, and since trading had stripped them of everything worthwhile that the Haida possessed, the ship hoisted anchor in Cloak Bay on the west coast of Langara Island and made for the southwest, "tacking occasionally during the night."

During the afternoon of July 5 several canoes of strangers came out from shore. The men in the canoes had valuable cloaks and were eager to trade. But unlike the previous island traders, these people wanted basins, kettles and pans, all of which were "most esteemed by these people".

The first village sighted by Dixon was probably in Guoy-skun, which stood at the head of Fury Bay, Langara Island. Still coasting south, he had realized "the natives did not live together in one social community, but were scattered about in different tribes, and probably at enmity with each other." About two in the afternoon of July 7 "being close in shore, we saw several canoes putting off, on which we shortened sail, and lay to for them, as the wind blew pretty fresh. The place these people came from had a very singular appearance, and on examining it narrowly, we plainly perceived that they lived in a very large hut, built on a small island, and well fortified after the manner of an hippah, on which account we distinguished this place by the name of Hippah Island."

The "hippah" was, according to some, the traditional house style of the Maori; according to others it was the English pronunciation of *o'pa*, the forts built by New Zealanders. The Haida name for the island was Nasto, meaning impregnable, which it was, judging from Beresford's next comment. "The tribe who inhabit this hippah, seem well defended by nature from any sudden assault of their enemies; for the ascent to it from the beach is steep, and difficult of access; and the other sides are well barricaded with pines and brushwood; notwithstanding which, they have been at infinite pains in raising additional fences of rails and boards; so that I should think they cannot fail to repel any tribe that should dare to attack their fortification." This is the first European description of a Haida fort or *t!aoj!i*. The nearby village was called Gatgainans.

"A number of circumstances," Beresford continued, "had occurred, since our first trade in Cloak Bay, which convinced us, that the natives at this place were of a more savage disposition, and had less intercourse with each other, than any Indians we had met with on the coast, and we began to suspect that they were cannibals in some degree. Captain Dixon no sooner saw the fortified hut just mentioned, than this suspicion was strengthened, as it was, he said, built exactly on the plan of the hippah of the savages at New Zealand. The people, on coming alongside, traded very quietly, and strongly importuned us by signs, to come on shore; at the same time giving us to understand (pointing towards the East) that if we visited that part of the coast, the inhabitants there would cut off our heads.

"I am not fond of hazarding conjectures, yet I cannot help remarking, that though the behaviour of these people was harmless and inoffensive, yet their attempt to persuade us to go on shore, is an additional proof in favour of our suspicion; they certainly wanted to decoy us to the hippah, and there, no doubt, we should have been instantly butchered."

In one of the canoes that came alongside the *Queen Charlotte* on July 9 there "was an old man, who appeared to have some authority over the rest, though he had nothing to dispose of; he gave us to understand, that in another part of these islands, (pointing to the Eastward) he could procure plenty of furs for us, on which Captain Dixon gave him a light horseman's cap: this present added greatly to his consequence, and procured him the envy of his companions in the other canoes, who beheld the cap with a longing eye, and seemed to wish it in their possession."

The old man's companions were not the only ones who had seen something they wanted. "There were likewise a few women amongst them, who all seemed pretty well advanced in years; their under lips were distorted in the same manner as those of the women at Port Mulgrave [Yakutat Bay], and Norfolk Sound [Sitka], and the pieces of wood were particularly large. One of these lip-pieces appearing to be peculiarly ornamented, Captain Dixon wished to purchase it, and offered the old woman to whom it belonged a hatchet; but this she refused with contempt; toes, basins, and several other articles were afterwards shown to her, and as constantly rejected.

"Our captain began now to despair of making his wished-for purchase, and had nearly given it up, when one of our people happening to show the old lady a few buttons, which looked remarkably bright, she eagerly embraced the offer, and was now altogether as ready to part with her wood ornament, as before she was desirous of keeping it. This curious lip-piece measured three and seven-eighth inches long, and two and five-eighth inches in the widest part: it was inlaid with a small pearly shell [abalone], round which was a rim of copper."

On July 25, 1787, after several days of desultory trading, sometimes as far as eight miles off the coast, the *Queen Charlotte* rounded a promontory and it being St. James Day, the rocky point was named Cape St. James.

"The morning of the 29th was moderate and cloudy; the wind being light and variable, we tacked occasionally, in order to stand well in with the shore, that no opportunity of trading might be lost. Towards noon the weather cleared up; our meridian observations gave 52 deg. 59 min. North latitude; so that we were near the middle of the island towards the northward and eastward. In this situation we saw high land to the northwest, near thirty leagues distant, and which evidently was the same we had seen on the 1st of July.

"Early in the afternoon we saw several canoes coming from shore, and by three o'clock we had no less than eighteen alongside, containing more than 200 people, chiefly men: this was not only the greatest concourse of traders we had seen, but what rendered the circumstance additionally pleasing, was the quantity of excellent furs they brought us, our trade now being equal, if not superior to that we met with in Cloak Bay, both in number of skins, and the facility with which the natives traded, so that all of us were busily employed, and our articles of traffic exhibited in the greatest variety."

One of the traders coming out to the ship was the old man encountered earlier. He had lost his hat in battle, and showed Captain Dixon and Beresford the wounds he had received in trying to keep his hat, and then asked for another, promising with signs that this time he would rather die than lose it.

"On our pointing to the eastward, and asking the old man whether we should meet with any furs there, he gave us to understand, that it was a different nation from his, and that he did not even understand their language, but was always at war with them; that he had killed great numbers, and had many of their heads in his possession.

"The old fellow seemed to take particular pleasure in relating these circumstances, and took uncommon pains to make us comprehend his meaning; he closed his relation with advising us not to come near that part of the coast for that the inhabitants would certainly destroy us. I endeavoured to learn how they disposed of the bodies of their enemies who were slain in battle; and though I could not understand the chief clearly enough positively to assert, that they are feasted on by the victors; yet there is too much reason to fear, that this horrid custom is practiced on this part of the coast; the heads are always preserved, as standing trophies of victory.

"Of all the Indians we had seen, this chief had the most savage aspect, and his whole appearance sufficiently marked him as a proper person to lead a tribe of cannibals. His stature was above the common size; his body spare and thin, and though at first sight he appeared lank and emaciated, yet his step was bold and firm, and his limbs apparently strong and muscular; his eyes were large and goggling, and seemed ready to start out of their sockets; his forehead deeply wrinkled, not merely by age, but from a continual frown; all this, joined to a long visage, hollow cheeks, high elevated cheek bones, and a natural ferocity of temper, formed a countenance not easily beheld without some degree of emotion: however, he proved very useful in conducting our traffic with his people, and the intelligence he gave us, and the methods he took to make himself understood, showed him to possess a strong natural capacity."

At Laskeek Bay Beresford had collected some 350 skins, "several racoon cloaks," a number of various-sized bladders of oil that "appeared to be of a most excellent kind for the lamp, [and] was perfectly sweet, and chiefly collected from the fat of animals." The next day the Haida returned, but this time brought with them only a few skins, all of which were of "an inferior quality," but as some of them had been fishing, they had halibut. These were quickly purchased by Beresford, "our fish having been expended some time."

About this same time the officers and crew of the *Queen Charlotte* realized that fish was about all the Haida had left to trade with, and since the period during which they were to have rendezvoused with Portlock and the *King George* at Nootka Sound had nearly slipped by, Dixon decided to leave the islands.

Something else had happened to hurry the *Queen Charlotte* on her way, something Beresford had been expecting. "Hitherto all the people we had met with at those islands, though evidently of a savage disposition, had behaved in a quiet orderly manner, but this evening they gave us a convincing proof of their mischievous disposition, and that in a manner which showed a considerable degree of cunning.

"The people who had got the halibut to sell, artfully prolonged their traffic more than was customary, and endeavoured by various methods, to engage our attention; in the mean time, several canoes paddled slyly astern, and seeing some skins piled against one of the cabin windows, one of the Indians thrust his spear through it, in order to steal the furs, but perceiving the noise alarmed us, they paddled away with precipitation; however, to make them sensible that we were able to punish attempts of this sort, even at distance, we fired several muskets after them, but did not perceive that they were attended with any fatal effects."

By noon on August 1 the ship was in sight of Cape St. James. A few hours later she was again approached by a Haida canoe with 14 people in it, but they had nothing to sell. Mainly their objective in approaching the *Queen Charlotte* was to tell Dixon that the gunfire on July 30 had killed one of the would-be thieves, but this did not matter: they wanted to remain friends. Since they had come alongside without any hesitation, Beresford tended to believe them. Others who believed such nonchalance would not be so lucky.

Two days later the ship was passing Cape St. James and Beresford began to sum up what had taken place during the past month. "There is," he wrote, "every reason to suppose, not only from the number of inlets we met with in coasting along the shore, but from our meeting the same inhabitants on the opposite sides of the coast, that this is not one continued land, but rather forms a group of islands; and as such, we distinguished them by the name of Queen Charlotte's Islands." [5]

Dixon Entrance was not named by Dixon. What happened was this: back in England in 1788, Dixon showed his chart of this area to Sir Joseph Banks, requesting "him to name such places as I had not filled up," so Banks, who had travelled with Cook on his first voyage and had become president of the Royal Society, "did me the honour to insert mine in the place you find it on the chart." [6]

Stowed away in the *Queen Charlotte's* hold were 1,821 sea otter skins bought from the Haida. Except for the shots fired at the Haida, there had been no problems with the islanders. The intelligent and sensible Dixon had kept most of his crew armed and on deck while Haida were in the vicinity, but there is no way to say this made any difference. What did make some difference was that the Haida encountered by Dixon allowed their chiefs to do the trading for them.

TWO BAD APPLES

Trading in the islands was rarely this peaceful again. In April 1791, about 150 Haida managed to board the *Gustavus* at Cloak Bay, ostensibly to trade. But Captain Thomas Barnett noticed that the women were returning to shore "and a great clamour arose," so he sent men aloft with blunderbusses and armed the men on deck with pistols. The Haida then calmed down and "trade went Briskere than Ever". [7]

Captain John Kendrick's various problems with the Haida are well documented—from the European side. The account of his best-known encounter was reported by 16-year-old John Boit, fifth mate of the *Columbia* on her second voyage. "Captain Kendrick inform'd us that he had had a skirmish, with the Natives at Barrell's sound in Queen Charlotte Isles, and was oblig'd to kill upwards of 50 of them before they wou'd desist from the attack. It appear'd to me, from what I cou'd collect that the Indians were the aggressors." [8]

This engagement took place in July 1791 and may have been due to Kendrick's drinking, but was more likely because of a chief's wish for revenge. In an encounter a year earlier, Kendrick had humiliated Koyah (also spelt Coya, Kower, Kouyer), a chief of the southernmost Haida, who was described as a "little diminutive savage looking fellow." In this altercation the Haida had stolen some small things—including some of Kendrick's underwear—from the *Lady Washington*, of which Kendrick was now in command, having traded ships with Robert Gray. Kendrick had taken Koyah and another chief hostage, chained them to gun carriages, and held them until the items were returned. When they were, instead of releasing Koyah, Kendrick "tied a rope round his neck, whipt him, painted his face, cut off his hair, took away from him a great many skins, and turned him ashore." [9]

With Koyah thus publicly shamed, his followers dropped away like flies. When Kendrick returned in June 1791, Koyah must have thought his time had come, so, after he convinced former followers that the *Lady Washington* could be theirs with little effort, they took the ship. Koyah was beside himself, and is said to have laughed at Kendrick, saying "Now put me into your gun carriage."

Kendrick and his crew fought back and the result was as described by Boit. The incident was recorded in a song, which became British Columbia's first ballad.

This anonymous doggerel was first printed in the 1830s but was certainly put together by someone aboard the *Lady Washington* in 1791. It begins:

Come all ye bold Northwestermen who plough the raging main,
Come listen to my story, while I relate the same;
'Twas of the Lady Washington decoyed as she lay,
At Queen Charlotte's Island, in North America.

moves on to the dramatic action:

Our powder we got ready and gun room open lay,
Our soul's we did commit to God prepar'd for a wat'ry grave!
We then informed our captain, saying ready now are we,
He says a signal I will give, it shall be "follow me."

and comes to an end seven stanzas later:

And now for to conclude, and make an end unto my son,
Success to the commander of the Lady Washington.
Success unto his voyages wherever he may go,
And may death and destruction always attend his foe. [10]

Only months after this second encounter with Kendrick, Koyah is reported to have led a large war-party against the chief of Skidegate, one of the long-standing enemies of the Kunghit people. In the summer of 1794 he and two other chiefs attacked and took an unnamed American vessel; all but one of the 11-man crew was killed. Details of what happened to the ship and its survivor were later reported by John Boit.

"Young likewise inform'd me that Old Capt. [Simon] Metcalfe," one of the first American traders to reach the islands, "in a Brig from the Isle of France had been cut of at Coyar's, in ye Queen Charlotte Isles by ye Natives of that place & ev'ry soul murder'd except one man who got up in ye Main top & was taken alive. Capt. Metcalfe's younger son was mate of the Brig. This man whom ye Natives took alive was afterwards bought of by ye Master of a Boston ship who pass'd here [Hawaiian Islands] about a fortnight since." [11]

It would seem, doubling back a bit, "that some time in the year '94 Capt. Metcalf came to an anchor in his Brig at Coyar's Sound & began a friendly traffic for furs with the Savages, but not being much suspicious of them, let a great number come upon his decks & the natives taken advantage of their superiority in numbers, clinch'd and stab'd, ev'ry man on board, except yet one that sprung up the Shrouds. This horrid Massacre was executed in the space of a few minutes with no loss, on the side of the natives. The man said that after they had insulted the body's of ye dead as they thought sufficiently, they told him to come down, which he accordingly did & deliver'd himself up to them, at the same time begging for mercy.

"They immediately took him on shore at the Village, where he was kept in the most abject slavery for about a twelve month. In the winter & in the worst of weather admist Snow & ice, they would drive him into ye Woods, to fetch logs & when he had got most to ye Village with his load, he would be met, by his task masters, who would disburthen him & drive him back after more & when any Vessell came into the harbour they would lash him hand & foot to a tree & keep him in that situation with a scanty allowance till she again sail'd for fear that he might run away." [12]

Koyah was not done. That fall Koyah and his men overran a British vessel and slaughtered her crew. In 1795 he led an attack against the *Union*, commanded, ironically, by John Boit. Now 19, he had returned to Houston Stewart Channel to trade. When attacked by Koyah and 300 of his men, Boit ordered the fire that killed the chief and 40 of his followers. Ninstints would be the next powerful chief in the area.

The sailors on the American and British vessels were not the only unlucky traders to visit the Kunghit people. Kendrick told Archibald Menzies, surgeon-botanist on Captain George Vancouver's surveying voyage to the North Pacific that while "in a port near the South end of Queen Charlotte's Isles (he saw) the remains of a Vessel of about 50 or 60 tons burthen that had been burnt down to the Water's edge, & from the appearance of the wood of some of her Timbers he conceivd it probable that she had been either built or repaird in some part of the East Indies, but for any further knowledge of what she was—the cause of her unfortunate destruction—or the fate of her unhappy Crew he could find nothing about her...the Indians, all of them he questioned declard, that she had drifted into the Harbour in that state from sea, in the night time, & that they neither saw nor knew anything of her till next morning." [13]

Kendrick told Menzies that he did not believe the Haida because of the state and situation of the wreck. He thought it likely that the ship, which remains unidentified, had been taken by the Indians and burned after everything removable was ashore. "Dead men tell no tales" might serve as a Haida motto in cases such as this.

By the time of Koyah's death in 1795, the Haida had guns which they occasionally used as well as did European sailors; alcohol had been introduced as an item of trade by the French ship *La Flavie* in 1791, and prostitution was part of the trading process, but some captains were not in favour of it. John Hoskin, second mate of the *Lady Washington* in July 1791, wrote that somewhere in the neighbourhood of Rose Harbour, on the southern shore of Houston Stewart Channel, about 20 Haida men and women came out to the ship and came aboard. The women were "ready and willing to gratify the amorous inclinations of any who wish it". [14] Captain Gray put an end to this side of the fur trade that day before it started.

VISITORS COME ABOARD

Koyah was a bad apple and Kendrick only marginally better; his moodiness was made bleaker by drink. More even-tempered visitors met equally well-adjusted Haida and were fascinated by them. Near Langara Island an unnamed man came aboard from a canoe to visit the explorer Jacinto Caamano in 1792. Caamano invited the fellow and a friend to supper and "They ate of all that was on the table, showing no sign of dislike of anything, or wishing first to taste it; and were more at home in the management of fork and spoon than any Spanish squireen. They drank wine and spirits at first sight; and, altogether, their behaviour seemed to point to a considerable inter-course with Europeans." [15]

Caamano's supper with his two visitors may have been an exception or, as is more likely, since the Haida were constantly at odds with each other, European-Haida relationships varied from village to village. Captain Richard Jeffry Cleveland, captain of the *Caroline*, who visited the islands in 1799, reported a colourful but brief meeting with another islander. When Cleveland reached the "Skittigates....a numerous and warlike tribe, whose intercourse with foreigners had been great, and to whose hostility and treachery some of them had fallen victims, there was a necessity for the observance of all that vigilance on our part, to guard against surprise, that we had been in the practice of observing. One of this tribe, in order to decoy men ashore, covered himself in a bear's skin, and came out of the border of the wood, on all fours, abreast the ship, while a party lay in ambush ready to fire on those who should come in pursuit. The strat-agem would have succeeded, had not one of the natives been too earnest to come forward, so as to be discovered in time for the boat to retreat, before any mischief had occurred.

"Soon after anchoring a canoe came to us, from which we procured three skins. The Indians in this canoe assured us that there were plenty of skins at the village, and manifested a desire that we should go there. In the morning of the 21st, several canoes came to us with some of the inferior chiefs. They were very urgent in their entreaties for us to go up to the village, alleging that it was so far for them to come....Towards evening a canoe came to us with the son of the chief of the Skittigates on board, who told us that if we would remain, his father would come to us, and bring a great many skins. In the night, which was perfectly calm, we heard frequent and wild howlings at the village, and occasionally the report of a musket.

"The morning of the 23d was calm, and a favorable current for the Indians to come to us; but, having waited till near noon without seeing a single canoe moving, we were at a loss to conjecture the reason, more especially after the promise of the king's son, last evening.

"The next day, when about two leagues south of Point Rose, the breeze not being sufficient to enable us to stem the current, we came to anchor. Soon afterwards, two large canoes came to us, in one of which was a young, good-looking warrior, the son-in-law of Coneyaw, who is head chief of the Tytantes tribe, and who, with other warriors, had come over on a hostile expedition against Cummashaw's tribe. Being so nearly on the point of leaving the coast, and therefore fearing no bad consequences from an exposure of our weakness, I acceded to the earnest solicitations of this young warrior to come on board.

"This was only one of the natives whom we had admitted on board since being on the coast. We invited him into the cabin, and gave him a glass of wine, which pleased him so much that he soon asked for another. Having made me a present of a very fine skin, I made a return of a shirt, jacket, and pantaloons, which he immediately put on, and appeared to be well satisfied with the figure he made, and much pleased with the dress. But the friendly feelings I had inspired suffered a momentary interruption, by my careless and apparently rude manner of giving him a handkerchief.

"Being on the opposite side of the cabin from that on which I was sitting, I threw it into his lap, which, instead of taking, he allowed to roll down on the floor, his feelings so much wounded that he actually shed tears; nor was it without considerable effort, that we persuaded him that no insult was intended, by assuring him that it arose from my ignorance of the etiquette which custom had established among them. This little interruption to our harmony was of short duration, the party aggrieved being satisfied with my apology; and having purchased from him and his comrades about sixty skins, we parted with mutual good-will and friendship."

Several days later "near to the village on North Island. A number of canoes soon came off, in one of which was the chief Coneyaw, and in another Eltargee. The latter had, a year or two ago, accidentally, it was said, caused the death of a Captain Newberry, by the discharge of a pistol, which he did not know was loaded. His looks, however, were so much against him, and, in the short intercourse we had with him, his actions and manner so corresponded with his looks, that I should require the clearest evidence to be satisfied that the disaster was purely the effect of accident." [16]

CONSIDERATIONS

Various explanations have been offered regarding the problems between the Haida and the Europeans. Certainly it was due to greed on both sides, but this is not the only answer, nor should the maritime fur traders be held entirely to blame. Except for Skedans, which apparently served as a trading centre not only among the Haida, but also for Tsimshian traders from the mainland, the Queen Charlotte Islands were not a peaceful country. Clans warred, as did villages, families and individuals. The situation as reflected in the ships' logs of the time may be read in various ways. Read one way and the Haida are seen as having lost their fear and respect for Europeans. Read another way and the Haida can be observed fighting for space on islands where the necessities of life were abundant only to those who owned the best salmon streams and clam beds, berry fields and kelp beds.

Read a third way and it is possible to see the Haida coming to terms with change. Some had learned that piracy paid, others that manners and peace were the way of the future. Women were prostitutes because traders and their crews expected them to be prostitutes. The men drank because Europeans drank. Items were stolen by certain Haida out of curiosity and because, undoubtedly, the Europeans stole from the villages they visited. It was a time of drastic change in the islands, not only for the Haida but for the Europeans who dealt with the Haida.

CHAPTER FIVE

EUROPE CASTS ITS SHADOW

CHANGING PATTERNS

IN SOME unnamed Queen Charlotte Island inlet in 1795, the Haida attacked a watering party from the British barque *Phoenix*. One British sailor died. In retaliation, Captain Hugh Moore brought the ship's cannon to bear on the village, but before the gunners could fire, the Haida cut loose with their own cannon. It is suspected this cannon was part of the loot from the *Resolution*, captured and burned by Haida pirates the previous summer. The shore fire was effective and the *Phoenix* beat a retreat, never to bother those particular Haida again.

Within the next decade the Haida would take more ships and kill more Europeans. West-coast Indians at Nootka Sound would slaughter the crew of the *Tonquin*, though it was a temporary survivor who torched the powder in the hold and killed dozens of the pirates, even while destroying himself and the ship. On the mainland the Tsimshian were also fighting back, as were the Alaska Haida and their Tlingit neighbours. About this same time the Tlingit burned Baranov's fort at Sitka Sound. Ship after ship went home from the Northwest Coast with stories of battles won or lost. To some it began to sound as though the coastal peoples were learning to hold their own.

But this was not to be. Something peculiar was happening. Witness the following event at Kaigani, a Haida village on Dall Island in Alaska. It was 1799, the two prisoners were Haida from the

Queen Charlotte Islands being handed over to a Kaigani Haida execution party by Americans, and the writer was William Sturgis, a 17-year-old sailor. Scotseye was a Cumshewa chief. He and his brother had murdered and scalped six Americans in the islands.

"The 12th of May was the day fixed upon for the execution, and notice was given for the whole Kigarnee tribe to assemble....The clear, deep blue Northern sky...was unobscured by the slightest cloud or vapour, and it was altogether as lovely a morning as ever shone....Before mid-day nearly the whole tribe, some 1,880 to 2,000 souls, made their appearance in canoes off the point of entrance and gliding silently into the cove arranged themselves at the head of it in a semi-circle...six or seven tiers deep, the women and children in the larger ones nearest the shore, the men, in those of a smaller size, taking a place near the centre.

"The scene was impressive....The ships, moored nearly in a line across the entrance...[all] occupation suspended, and the men aloft upon the yards and rigging—more than 300 canoes filled with Indians in full dress, the faces of the men painted in war style, and all standing or sitting in their canoes as immoveable and silent as the rocks and trees beyond them....At this moment, a large war canoe struck out from the circle and slowly approached the centre ship. Two young slaves, one at each end, moved and guided the canoe—about halfway from the stern to the centre, and facing the prow, stood Keow, drawn up to his full height of more than six feet, his arms rolled in a rich fur robe and folded across his breast. At a like distance from the prow, and facing the stern, stood the two executioners, Quoltlong and Kilchart, the nephew and brother of Keow....the prisoners were brought upon deck and silently passed over the side. I stood near them at the moment, Scotsi [Scotseye], the elder, was grave, but unmoved; while a prisoner on board the ship he had, at times, appeared somewhat dejected. Not so with his brother. He had, from the first, shown a bold, unflinching spirit....He gloried in what he had done [killing American sailors] and declared that he only regretted his fate as it prevented him from more fully avenging the injuries inflicted upon his family and friends by the white men.

"As he passed over the side he threw a glance of scornful defiance upon those around him, and met Keow and the executioners with an undaunted look. The chiefs (Scotsi and his brother) were roped together by one arm of each. They were seated in the canoe immediately in front of the executioners, and facing Keow, who glared at them with a look of suppressed fury, which was boldly returned by the younger captive. The canoe moved slowly from the ship some 50 yards to a point nearly central, and stopping, all remained a few moments in a death-like silence, when Keow, turning his face, gave the fatal signal.

"Both victims were struck at the same instant, and with such force that the blows were distinctly heard on board the ships....The executioners raised their daggers in the air....Upon the deep silence of the moment broke forth a yell that sent a thrill of terror through the stoutest heart and might well appal the boldest spirit. The war hoop from a single voice is not soon forgotten, but when a thousand join to give it utterance, under the influence of the wildest passion, it can be compared with no earthly sound. It rolled upwards and reverberated from the mountain to mountain until it seemed to fill all space." [1]

Realistic as this description is, the author missed the most important detail. This moment, more than any other in the recorded history of the Haida, marks the point when certain Haida decided their future was European and the old ways were no longer viable. It was a turning point from which there would be no return.

By 1795 the maritime fur trade was dominated by Americans (of the 50 ships known to have traded in the islands between 1795 and 1825, 41 were American, seven British, and two Russian) who were quite willing to do what they had to in pursuit of furs. This included selling firearms and whisky to the Haida, encouraging prostitution, and playing an active role in the Northwest Coast slave trade.

Most of this is revealed again and again in the diary kept by Stephen Reynolds, a member of the crew of the *New Hazard*, which was on the coast for 18 months in 1811 and 1812. It is almost the complete opposite of Beresford's record of the *Queen Charlotte's* time in the same vicinity 24 years earlier. Women, slaves, alcohol, firearms and the endless brutality—all the details are reported, albeit briefly, but these are not the central theme of Reynolds' story. What lies at the core of this account is so mundane it—the type of trade goods— appears unimportant until the full impact of what Reynolds is saying sinks in.

The *New Hazard* and the ships working the coast were little more than travelling shopping marts. One week they might be at Nootka Sound, the next in Alaskan waters. When the *New Hazard* ran short of supplies she made a hurried trip to Hawaii for fresh stock. As well as the iron implements that were stock trade items, the *New Hazard* carried "musquets, bread, molasses, sugar, India cottons, wearing apparel, hardware, gunpowder, paints, iron, rice, sheetings, shot, tobacco, wollens, woodenware." [2] At least one of the ships on the coast at this time hired Indian hunters, some of whom remained on board long enough to make one trip to California and thence to China. Another ship appears to have served as some sort of American ferry, moving supplies and men between Astoria (Fort George until it changed hands during the War of 1812) and the northern portion of the Northwest Coast.

Although the details of much of this are unknown, the trading goods would certainly have made some, if not all, of the Queen Charlotte Island Haida dependent on European supplies. Simultaneously, these trade goods, and the necessity of securing vast numbers of furs, would have disrupted the traditional Haida year; subsistence now depended on furs, not on hunting and gathering activities. In turn, the demand for furs made hunters—whatever their ancestry—rich, thus putting the class system out of kilter.

Now, considering the execution of the two Haida by a rival chief in the light of the changing patterns of Haida life, it may be that the Kaigani Haida were consolidating their business relationship with the maritime fur traders. It was certainly clear to them by this time that without the traders, they would have to return to a way of life that was now repugnant. Worse, given the Northwest Coast Indian's sense of pride, it meant the Kaigani would lose face, an unthinkable situation.

But everyone on the islands knew that the fur trade was winding down. Only three ships are known to have traded with the Haida in 1825, although a fourth was sighted in the vicinity of Skidegate. In fact, only 12 ships are known to have reached the British Columbia coast that year. The maritime fur trade south of Kaigani was over, and it must have looked to the Haida as though their new-found prosperity was gone with it.

THE COMPANY MOVES UPCOAST

There was good news in the offing. However, even had the Haida known that the *William & Ann*, the last ship to visit Cumshewa and Skidegate in 1825, belonged to the Hudson's Bay Company, it would have meant nothing to them. The arrival of this ship was the harbinger of a new stage in the maritime fur trade.

Activity had not ceased on the coast, but what there was was a long way from the islands. Alexander Baranov had re-established Sitka in 1804, but to trade there meant a long voyage. There was

Fort George near the mouth of the Columbia River, and the Russian post of Fort Ross even farther south. For a while the Haida were saved by a smattering of trading vessels that wandered into their vicinity; the *Volunteer* was there in 1829 with Reverend Jonathan Green aboard, and other ships undoubtedly came and went, leaving no record. According to a smattering of evidence recorded by Marius Barbeau, during this time various far-sighted Haida began to trade along the coast, possibly as far south as the Columbia River. If so, then certain Haida businessmen possessed their own ships, which is not surprising; according to some stories the Haida had been sailing aboard American and British ships for decades. When there were no traders to sell the skins to, the Haida took them to Sitka, where there was a ready market.

Realizing that the Boston- and London-based traders in the maritime fur trade were leaving the business, and knowing that the Russians at Sitka were still prospering, the HBC began moving upcoast from Fort Vancouver. Fort Langley was established on the lower Fraser River in 1827. In 1831-32 the company built Fort Simpson at the mouth of the Nass River, and established both Fort Nisqually near present-day Tacoma, Washington and Fort McLoughlin on Milbanke Sound near Bella Bella in 1833. To maintain their lifestyle, the Haida begin visiting these southern forts and since the Kwakiutl from northern Vancouver Island found their way to Fort Langley, undoubtedly the Haida were there too.

Trustworthy details of this period do not exist. This is a time in island history when the Haida are usually described as an insular people who were lured away from their villages and traditional way of life. It is highly improbable that this was so. By the 1830s the Haida had been dependent to varying degrees on European goods for 40 years. Many had visited Russian Sitka, others had visited HBC forts; some had sailed to Japan, China and Britain; given the number of argillite carvings dating from this time, and the island business of supplying canoes to the Tsimshian, at least a few Haida were prosperous artisans; there were also the Haida farmers who supplied potatoes to the visiting ships and to Fort Simpson; a people with this record are not lured away from home because whisky, baubles and beads are waved in front of their faces. Instead, the Haida were making these trips because they wanted to maintain their European lifestyle.

In 1825 the appearance of the *William & Ann* at Skedans marked the second dramatic turning point in island history in the 19th century. From existing records it appears that the arrival of the HBC's *William & Ann*, was the company's first direct contact with the islands. Thanks to Dr. John Scouler, the ship's surgeon, there is a record of what the HBC found there.

The ship reached the islands on June 23 and began trading almost immediately. "This afternoon [June 24]....We passed what we took to be an Indian village, & were not dissapointed, for a canoe came of[f] to us. They informed us that the name of their village was Skedans. They had all of them blankets, & their hats were of a much neater shape & displayed far more ingenuity than those of the Cheenooks [Chinook were a Columbia River people]. They were also well supplied with fire arms....Their conduct was bold and decided, bordering on ferocity, & while on board they behaved with the utmost selfishness."

After a trip to the mainland, particularly Observatory Inlet, to trade with the Tsimshian, the *William & Ann* returned to the islands on July 26. "In the afternoon we were of[f] Skittigass & afforded us an opportunity of sending our interpreter ashore. Although in one respect he dissapointed our hopes by stealing when he had the opportunity of doing it; we ought not to judge of him with the same severity as we would do of those who know better.

"The acuteness of the Queen Charlotte's Islanders has prompted them to adopt a great many customs of civilized life, & the cultivation of potatoes is very general among them, and had our time admitted of it we might have obtained any quantity of this useful vegetable. This consideration alone, in my opinion, places them far above the natives of the Columbia in the scale of intelligence. With all the advantage of having Europeans constantly among them I do not know of one improvement requiring the smallest exertion that has been adopted by the Cheenooks. Poor Skittigass Tom [the interpreter] was the only Indian that ever expressed much anxiety to learn to read and write, & was very fond of obtaining a few ciphers. He made charts of Nass & Skittigass, which served to give a very good idea of the coast & of the different tribes settled along it."

Later Scouler wrote that traditionally the Haida, particularly those of Masset, Skidegate and Cumshewa, were some of the wealthiest people on the coast, but that was before the depletion of the sea otter. In "order to procure blankets," the Haida Scouler saw were forced to "fabricate most of the curiosities found on the coast, but their staple article is the potato, which they sell in great quantities to the mainland tribes." [3]

Village of Cumshewa in 1878. (COURTESY GEOLOGICAL SURVEY OF CANADA)

Back in the islands, the first visiting American who was not a fur trader had arrived. This was Reverend Green, aboard the *Volunteer* out of the Hawaiian Islands, and though he would be impressed by the appearance of the islands, the people he first encountered left him gripping his Bible all the harder.

On April 10, 1829, he wrote: "Today, it being rainy, the cabin has been filled with Indians. The sensation which I experience at such times, arising from the heat and effluvia, are well nigh insupportable. Among others, there were present two chiefs belonging to the Shebasha [Tsimshian] tribe. They speak the Nass language. About six weeks since, a party of the Kumshewa [Cumshewa] Indians, from Queen Charlotte's Island, visited the Shebasha tribe for the purpose of trade. In the course of their negotiation a dispute arose, when the Shebasha men attacked the Kumshewa party, and killed several of them. The residue fled, but in crossing over to the island others were drowned. This intelligence being communicated to the tribe, the Kumshewa men prepared to take vengeance. They immediately went over to seek redress, but, ere they arrived, the Shebasha tribe had abandoned their village, and started for this place. Their houses were demolished, and their property, which was left behind, carried off. How greatly do these bloody men need the gospel."

"This morning we found ourselves near Queen Charlotte's Island," Green wrote 12 days later. "We came down opposite the Kumshewa village, and several of the Indians came off to us: This is the tribe, several of whom were killed by the Shebasha men. Some of the sufferers in that quarrel were on board. One lost a child, another a sister, another his wife, besides receiving a wound himself. Their badge of mourning is a face painted horribly black, with their hair cut very short. I told them my object, and endeavored to show them the happiness of living in peace with their fellow men."

On June 24, Green wanted to go ashore, but did not; his diary tells the story. Several of the men at Skidegate "appeared pleased, and most earnestly solicited me to go on shore. They offered four or five of their principal men as hostages, and they repeatedly assured me that all would be well. Though I am anxious to see the country and visit this village, yet I am not quite clear that I ought to go. I could not effect much by a single visit, and there are too many chiefs here, to ensure safety from the fact of having on board a hostage."

A day later Green wrote that the people of Skidegate were both tiresome and troublesome. One reason for this was "that their skins are the sea otter, there being very little land fur on the island. One of these skins is worth more than ten beavers, and being scarce and eagerly sought, the man who has taken one calculates to barter at least two days before he sells it, and during this time he claims special privileges, expects that he shall have free access to the cabin to eat, drink, and lounge, and he must have things in style, too, or he will be highly offended."

Skidegate, it was Green's opinion, was a small village of less than 500 people. He thought them more sedentary than the other Haida he had encountered; "they manufacture from grass, hats of an excellent quality....pipes, which they make of a kind of slatestone....[and they were] fierce for trade, bringing for sale fish, fowls, eggs, and berries, and [offered] them in exchange for tobacco, knives, spoons, carpenter's tools...buttons and clothes." [4]

Disaster struck the next HBC vessel to trade in the islands. First the schooner *Vancouver*, under Captain Alexander Duncan, was damaged on the rocks near the entrance to Portland Canal in 1831. It was this accident that caused the company to purchase the *Llama* from Captain William H. McNeill, an American, whom they promptly hired to command his former vessel. Three years later the *Vancouver* was hit by a storm and went aground on Rose Spit, where she broke up, but not before she was salvaged by the Haida, a bit of business not appreciated by the HBC.

Rose Spit is a sandspit extending from Rose Point on the north-eastern corner of Graham Island in a north-north-easterly direction for almost three miles. It is one of the most dramatic dangers to ships on the east coast of the Queen Charlotte Islands. Nai-kun, The Long Nose of Nai, is the Haida name for the point and its spit. Captain William Douglas of the *Iphigenia* gave it its present name in 1788 in honour of George Rose, a British M.P. and writer interested in the maritime fur trade. On Robert Gray's charts it is Cape Lookout and on Joseph Ingraham's it is variously Sandy Point and Masset Spit. In 1792 Jacinto Caamano, captain of the *Anazazu*, named it Punta Invisible, a name Captain Vancouver rendered Punta Ymbisible on his charts.

The next visitor to leave a record of his time in the islands was John Work, a chief trader with the Hudson's Bay Company; like his contemporaries John Tod, Peter Skene Ogden and James Douglas, he knew the west, having spent his life on the Pacific Slope, from Russian Alaska to Spanish California. Work spent the first ten months of 1835 aboard the *Llama*, the HBC brig commanded by Captain McNeill.

On Sunday, May 10, 1835, Work opened his diary to write: "Showry squally weather....In the course of the day a considerable number of the Skidegate Indians came off, and supplied us with some fish & a bear skin and a few Martens.

"There was such a jabble of the sea on, that the canoes could not lay along side & they had to go ashore. The Indians were shy to come aboard for some time till they were told they had nothing to fear. Their shyness arose, from the loss of the *Vancouver* last year, as they are connected with the tribe who inhabit where she was lost, and who plundered her. We learn from them that 25 Canoes of that tribe and these people are off now at the fort Simpson for the purpose of making up matters, and that the Chief means to exculpate himself & his people by stating that it was not their fault, but the fault of the waves that occasioned the loss of the vessel. This appears to be their way of reasoning on the subject. They have also taken some things with them to the fort. These people say they have few furs, that those who have gone to the fort have taken what furs they had with them, but that another tribe the Cawwilth [Chaatl], which live a little farther up the Sound have got some furs.

"Monday, May 11. Showry weather....Indians visited us during the day and traded 6 or 8 bear skins and about 40 Martens and 1 land Otter, which is probably the most of what they have got. We also bought some potatoes, for which we paid higher than usual for, but they are scarce now, and I much want these for seed at the fort. A few of the Cawelth men were also here, but had very little with them. They have two Sea Otters which they are to bring tomorrow. These people appear very poor; they are wretchedly clothed and apparently badly off for every thing ....This formerly used to be one of the best places for Sea Otters on the coast, but now scarcely any is to be found among them. They grow a considerable quantity of potatoes [and] they have several patches under cultivation about their villages." [5]

Another reason, noted by Work, for the drastically changing trading conditions was that any number of the Haida had sailed as hunters on ships bound for California and back via Hawaii; they knew what the skins were worth and expected the same prices from the HBC as they did from the Americans.

Work was based at Fort Simpson, now Port Simpson, which was built after abandoning a fort of the same name near the mouth of the Nass River. He was there from 1834 until the late 1840s and during his tenure, he took a census, dating from 1836 to 1841, of the Haida villages. This census lists 13 villages: Lu-lan-na, Nigh-tasis, Massette, Ne-coon, A-se-guang, Skid-de-gates, Cum-sha-was, Skee-dans, Quee-ah, Cloo, Kish-a-win, Kow-welth, and Too; by his count the population of the islands was 6,693.

Lu-lan-na, actually the villages of Yaku and Kiusta, was a town with 20 houses and a population of 80 men, 76 women, and 140 children. Nigh-tasis was an early 19th-century village that stood where Kung would be built later in the century; it had 15 houses and a population of 280. Massette or Masset was a huge village of 160 houses and a total population of 2,473. The village of Ne-coon or Naikoon was small, only five houses and a population of 122; now almost legendary due to its having been abandoned and then covered by drifting sand, it was known to the Haida as Point-Town Village. Hlgihla-ala is today the name of the village referred to by Work as A-se-guang, a place with nine houses and 120 inhabitants. It was located near Cape Ball. Skid-de-gates, or Skidegate, was the islands' second-largest town with 48 houses and 738 inhabitants. Cum-sha-was was better known as Cumshewa; its name was derived from a Bella Bella word referring to the riches—herring, eulachon, salmon—at the mouth of a river, and it was one of the last Moresby Island villages to be abandoned. Its last residents moved to Skidegate. Skee-dans was the lovely village of Skedans or Koona. Work counted 30 houses there and 439 residents. Quee-ah is Ninstints, the southern-most of Haida villages; Quee-ah refers to Koyah, a descendant of the Koyah killed by the *Union's* gunfire in 1795. In Work's account the town consisted of 20 houses and 308 inhabitants. Cloo is Tanu or Klue, a village of 40 houses and 545 people. Kish-a-win or Kaisun had 18 houses and 329 inhabitants, and like Kow-welth, now Chaatl, with its 35 houses and 561 people, it was among the first major villages to be abandoned. The last village on Work's census list was Too. Better known as Tian, it was a town of ten houses and 196 people. Tian was reported deserted apparently by the late 1850s, for unknown reasons.

In the "Journal of Events" kept at Fort Simpson between 1835 and 1837 there is mention of the Masset Haida visiting the fort 12 times, and the Haida of Cumshewa and Skidegate visiting 19 times. Due to the weather, most of these trips were made between March and September and the Haida came to trade potatoes for such necessities as blankets, calico and tobacco, rifles and rum.

Poor trading conditions, and the danger to sailing vessels in the virtually uncharted waters and cramped passages, led to a revolution in the fur trade. Governor George Simpson, the general superintendent of the HBC in North America, decided that instead of at forts along the coast, trading should be conducted from ship-board. And while shipboard would continue to mean vessels like the *Llama*, it would include the newly built *Beaver*, which was, even as Work left the islands, being fitted in the River Thames. This change of direction meant that the northern forts such as Taku in Alaska, and McLoughlin in British Columbia would someday have to be abandoned.

The *Beaver* reached Fort Simpson in June 1836. The next year she was back in the area and reached the Queen Charlotte Islands. Now she was under the command of Captain McNeill. That season, McNeill is said to have bought numerous furs, including beaver and mink, marten and lynx, elk and bear, with a variety of goods: axes, beads, knives, blankets, molasses, tobacco, files, and flints. This list sounds so similar to what the Haida had asked for 40 years earlier that it is probable the *Beaver* was trading in still-unexplored corners of Southeastern Alaska and at the headwaters of some of the more remote northern BC inlets.

Seven years after the *Beaver's* first trip north, in 1843, forts Taku and McLoughlin were torn down and everything salvageable moved to the southern tip of Vancouver Island. There James Douglas, soon to join Work and Ogden on the governing board of the Columbia District as Dr. John McLoughlin retired, started the construction of Fort Victoria. Along with Sitka, this place soon became a mecca for well-to-do Haida who could afford the trip south.

TWO CAPTAINS AND A LADY

At this point it is as though a black cloth is dropped over the Queen Charlotte Islands. The Haida came and went at Fort Simpson, at Fort Victoria and Fort Nisqually, deep in the heart of Puget Sound. Their reputation as terrible fighters grew, but these warriors and traders were just as well known for drinking and pimping and gambling, as were their European counterparts. Well recorded as some of these activities are in newspapers, journals and letters of the time, no details are known of what the Haida were actually doing on their visits.

If even the sketchiest outline of their activities existed—and the idea that they were continually up to no good is nothing more than century-old gossip—something might also be known of a Haida girl in love and a Haida chief who fascinated the few people to have personally encountered him.

Generally, Haida women were considered the most attractive of all the Northwest Coast peoples. Captain George E. Pickett, United States Army, was, like the HBC's Captain McNeill, one of the first whites to marry a Haida woman. Pickett married his lady sometime in the 1850s, while he was in command of Fort Bellingham. A West Point graduate and veteran of the Mexican War, Pickett first came to international attention while stationed on San Juan Island during the "Pig War," a confrontation that almost led to yet another clash of arms between the United States and Britain. For his efforts there Congress thanked him, but in 1861 Pickett resigned to join the Confederate Army. In 1863 his famous charge at Gettysburg has been called "the highwater mark of the Confederacy". When he left Fort Bellingham, he left James Tilton Pickett, his young son whose Haida mother had died during childbirth. The younger Pickett later became a well-known painter and illustrator in the Pacific Northwest.

About the time that Captain Pickett married his lady, another captain was making a name for himself. This was Captain John, the leading Haida chief on the Northwest Coast. Known as "the King of the Hydahs" in the late 1850s, he was described by a Victoria *Colonist* reporter as "about 40 years of age and above the average height of an Indian. His sallow face was surrounded by

Captain John and his son. (COLLECTION OF CHARLES LILLARD)

luxuriant black whiskers and his upper lip was adorned with a sweeping black moustache. His stature and his light complexion and the hirsute appendages gave rise to the impression that he was the son of a Russian."

That he may have been; it was said that he had spent two years in St. Petersburg, Russia; had lived in London, and could write English and speak Russian. He was, the reporter said, "the finest specimen of the Indian I ever met. He ruled his subjects arbitrarily, and it was death or severe punishment to any member of the tribe who might disobey his orders." [6]

Drink was said to have led him to his downfall, but he had not drunk anything stronger than water for most of his life. Why he started, if he did, is not known. Whatever happened, in 1860 Captain John was in the thick of things in Victoria Harbour when the *Royal Charlie* was fired on by some northern Indians. For his role in the affair the police arrested John and when he resisted arrest and drew a knife he was shot and killed.

What was happening in the Haida villages on the islands during the 1840s remains a mystery. In 1850 a corner of the black cloth was lifted briefly, and for the most unexpected reason, but only to cast light on the first episode of European history to take place on the islands, not on the sea around them.

GOLD

Gold was discovered on the islands. The discovery was first mentioned in a letter from James Douglas, soon to be the governor of the Crown Colony of Vancouver Island, to Archibald Barclay, the London-based secretary of the HBC.

"Another object of Mr. Works visit to this place [Fort Rupert, a trading post and coal mine at the north end of Vancouver Island] was to communicate intelligence of an important discovery lately made by the natives of the Queen Charlotte's Island, who have found Gold on the west coast of the Island, as far as we can gather from their reports, about Cape Henry Englefields Bay.

"They brought in a fine specimen of Gold in white Quartz, the same kind of rock which yields the rich harvest of the precious metal in Calefornia. This specimen was brought in by an Indian of a neighbouring tribe and not by the inhabitants of the Gold district, who were making a great secret of their newly discovered treasure.

"Our accounts of the discovery are in consequence derived from other Indians, who have not visited the District since the gold was discovered, and are somewhat conflicting in their details. Some say that the gold is found in rocks, while others assert that it is in the sand, in such small particles that it is difficult to pick up....This is all the information we have yet received about this important discovery but we soon expect further particulars as Mr. Work has dispatched Pierre Lagace one of the Company's servants with a party of Indians to examine the Gold District and he will take the first opportunity of going there himself with the Steam Vessel when she returns from Sitka." [7] Of this trip by Lagace to the islands, the most important outcome may have been the European discovery of Skidegate Channel, the narrow waterway separating Graham and Moresby islands.

Hubert Howe Bancroft, the only historian to interview men alive and active in British Columbia at the time, wrote that in 1851, "a native of the Queen Charlotte Islands appeared at Victoria with a bag of specimens.

"Writing Earl Grey the 29th of March 1851, Governor Blanshard [the first governor of Vancouver Island] says: 'I have heard that fresh specimens of gold have been obtained from the Queen Charlotte Islanders. I have not seen them myself but they are reported to be very rich....[the company] intends to send an expedition in the course of the summer to make proper investigations.' " [8] The *Huron* was the first ship with miners aboard sent to the goldfields by the company, ostensibly as a trading vessel. It returned with some gold-bearing quartz and about the same time a former mate of an Australian ship, *Georgiana*, working for the HBC, put together an exhibit in Olympia, Washington Territory, of gold he claimed to have found in the Queen Charlotte Islands. As a result, some American miners put together an expedition, but nothing came of it.

What is not generally known about the *Georgiana's* trip to the islands is that she went aground there. Helpless, the ship, her crew and passengers were captured and held hostage by the Haida. Although it was rumoured that she was ransomed by the HBC for $1,839 in trade goods, late in 1851 Douglas wrote to Barclay that "The sloop *Georgiana* was lately wrecked on Queen Charlottes Island, with 22 American Gold Hunters on board; the lives of the people were spared but all their property was seized by the Indians. We received that intelligence by a letter from the Master of the *Georgiana*, then a captive in the hands of the Indians, and an American vessel has been lately dispatched from Nesqually at the expense of the United States to the assistance." [9]

Next, the HBC sent the brigantine *Una* to the islands. The ship made two trips south with quartz, the ship's miners having discovered a vein some seven inches wide and 80 feet long. In some places this find was 25% gold. The value of the first shipload is not known; then on her second homeward trip the *Una* sank, taking her treasure with her. The *Recovery* went north with 30 miners and after three months of hard work, the miners realized enough gold to pay themselves wages of $30 a month. Captain McNeill was on the islands during the mining activity and filed a report to James Douglas. This is the only first-hand account of the rush and it makes clear the role the Haida were playing on their islands. Coming from McNeill these observations can be trusted, for he was not only an experienced trader, he was married to a Haida woman some think was a Kaigani chief.

"I am sorry to inform you that we were obliged to leave off blasting, and quit the place for Fort Simpson, on account of the annoyance we experienced from the natives. They arrived in large numbers, say 30 canoes, and were much pleased to see us on our first arrival. When they saw us blasting and turning out the gold in such large quantities, they became excited and commenced depredations on us, stealing the tools, and taking at least one-half the gold that was thrown out by the blast. They would lie concealed until the report was heard, and then make a rush for the gold; a regular scramble between them and our men would then take place; they would take our men by the legs, and hold them away from the gold. Some blows were struck on these occasions. The Indians drew their knives on our men often.

"The men who were at work at the vein became completely tired and disgusted at their proceedings, and came to me on three different occasions and told me that they would not remain any longer to work the gold; that their time was lost to them, as the natives took one-half of the gold thrown out by the blast, and blood would be shed if they continued to work at the digging; that our force was not strong or large enough to work and fight also. They were aware they could not work on shore after hostility had commenced, therefore I made up my mind to leave the place, and proceed to this place," wrote McNeill from the relative peace of Fort Simpson.

"The natives," he continued, "were very jealous of us when they saw that we could obtain gold by blasting; they had no idea that so much could be found below the surface; they said that it was not good that we should take all the gold away; if we did so, they would not have anything to trade with other vessels should any arrive. In fact, they told us to be off." [10]

Later that year the *Susan Sturgis* arrived at the site of the gold discoveries and the captain gathered up bits of quartz left by the miners aboard the *Una*. Consequently he sold this quartz for $1,500 in San Francisco. But the role of the *Susan Sturgis* in Queen Charlotte Island history was not over.

Twenty thousand dollars was said to be the grand sum taken from the islands during this rush, but how this figure was arrived at is not known. Judging from how few details are known about the mining activities of this period, $20,000 sounds like a wild estimate. At Fort Victoria, still curious about the possibilities of gold in the islands, Governor Douglas sent Major William Downie north; he wanted an expert's opinion and Downie was one of the best-known miners to emerge from the California gold rush.

Downie did not think much of the prospects in the islands. Writing years later, he had little to say about the place. "We were a band of twenty-seven miners, all old hands and well tried, and we steered our course for Gold Harbor on Moresby Island....We carefully examined a spot where a large quantity of gold had been taken out sometime before, but could not find anything worth working, although we saw quartz and did some blasting. The general nature of the rock was trap and hornblend, and, at the head of Douglas Inlet, we found granite, as well as slate, talcose rock and coal, but not gold; and I concluded, that the large amount of this metal, which had been found previously in those parts with so little difficulty, existed merely in what the miners call an off-shoot or blow-out, which can only be explained as one of those freaks of nature, so often found in a mining country.

"In the Skidegate Channel we met with but little better success. We were wind-bound for some time near the Casswer [Chaatl] Indian village, where we discovered traces of previous prospecting. Here the indications of gold were certainly more distinct. We met an old Indian Chief, who to accommodate us gave his name as Scotch Guy. He wore a large piece of gold, weighing probably two ounces, but he could not be persuaded to tell us where he found it....I received the impression, that the natives there are first-class prospectors, and know all about gold mining." [11]

Overall, this gold rush had little direct effect on the islands. Mitchell Inlet, known locally as Gold Harbour, was named in honour of Captain William Mitchell, the genial "Wullie" Mitchell, captain of the *Una* and various other HBC vessels. Georgiana Point is a reminder of the *Georgiana's* troubles in the area and Demariscove Point commemorates the *Demaris Cove*, the American ship sent north to free the Georgiana's crew and passengers. And far away in England the British government sent a letter to Governor Douglas, with whom it was none too pleased at the moment, as the HBC was doing little to promote or assist in the colonization of Vancouver Island. This letter, written in September 1852, made Governor James Douglas the lieutenant-governor of the Queen Charlotte Islands.

This commission, he was informed, "is issued solely to meet the circumstances of the times; it conveys to you no power to make laws or constitute a regular government; but it gives the party bearing it a position of authority as representing Her Majesty's government in the district, which is both important and valuable." Douglas's first and last act as lieutenant-governor, as far as is known, was to set up a system by which prospectors, American or otherwise, had to purchase mining licences. It was a forerunner of what Douglas would do in 1858 at the onset of the Fraser River gold rush. His proclamation of March 1853 said, in part, "all mines of gold, and all gold in its natural place of deposit within the colony of Queen Charlotte's Island" was British. [12] Shortly after this a British gunboat began surveying the coast of the islands.

Early in September 1852 the *Susan Sturgis* returned to the islands. Her captain, Matthew Rooney, traded along the east coast for fish, as he looked for Edenshaw, a Haida chief well known for his knowledge of the islands. With Edenshaw's help, Rooney reasoned, he would be able to trade anywhere on the islands, even in the unexplored inlets on the islands' west coast. Rooney found Edenshaw at Skidegate and promptly hired him and started for Kung, Edenshaw's village at the narrows separating Naden Harbour and Virago Sound.

No one really knows exactly what happened next. It is said that Chief Nestecanna of Skidegate warned Rooney that trouble was brewing and that Rooney paid him no attention. On the way to Kung, sometime not long after rounding Rose Point, the *Susan Sturgis* was met by Chief Weah. Rooney thought Weah was trading for fish; various Haida who were aboard claimed later that Weah came out to talk to Edenshaw, and Edenshaw told Weah that he was planning to take control of the *Susan Sturgis* as soon as she reached Kung.

There are several versions of what followed. The most thoughtful is this one. Chief Weah and his men came alongside the *Susan Sturgis* in 25 canoes. Supposedly Weah wanted to trade dried fish for whatever trade goods were on the vessel, but Rooney, a quite unperceptive man at the best of times, paid no attention to the fact that the faces of the men in the canoes were painted black—a sure sign of their hostile intentions. Also there were no women in the canoes and everyone knew that the Haida did little trading without their women. Rooney paid no attention to any of this and invited all 150 Haida aboard his ship. The next thing he and his men knew, they were naked and bound. Shivering from cold and fear, they watched as Weah and his men stripped the ship of everything of value, including $1,500 in gold and silver coin from the ship's strongbox. Edenshaw stood by and watched all this happen and did nothing, according to most accounts. And then the 150 warriors led by Chief Weah burned the *Susan Sturgis*.

Years later, Edenshaw told Reverend Collison, who probably knew him as well as anyone did in later life, that it was all the doing of Weah's men and "had he not been present the crew would all have been slaughtered." Edenshaw went on to say that the pirates had been ready to shoot Rooney and his crew when he "took them under his protection."

"On the other hand," Collison admitted, "some members of the tribe informed me that it was by this chief's [Edenshaw] orders that the schooner was attacked and taken. It is probable that both statements are true. These white men who had formed the crew were divested of their clothing, which was appropriated by their captors, and received blankets instead. Thus barefoot, and with scant clothing, they were enslaved by the chiefs, to whom they became hewers of wood and drawers of water. Thus they were retained as slaves, until redeemed by the Hudson's Bay Company, who paid over to the chiefs a number of bales of blankets for their release." [13]

Another version of this story says that on September 26, 1852, off Masset Harbour Rooney wrote a plea "To Whatever Christian This May Come" saying: "This is to inform the public that the Captain and the crew of the schooner *Susan Sturgis* are now confined in the after cabin of said vessel, the tribe of Masset Indians having taken the ship this day at 10 A.M. and are now fighting with Edenshaw and a few of his men who are trying to save our lives." [14]

At any rate, by October 10 Rooney and his crew, minus one crewman unaccountably left at Masset, were at Fort Simpson. There, it is said, the HBC ransomed Rooney for $250 in blankets and each crew member for $30 in the same commodity. The story is not entirely clear; when later questioned by Captain Augustus Kuper, commander of the H.M.S. *Thetis* in Victoria, Rooney was not able to add further details.

A year later, on July 5, 1853, the H.M.S. *Virago* reached Masset Harbour for the expressed purpose of punishing the guilty parties. Governor Douglas suggested that, if nothing else, the navy level the town of Masset and destroy all the canoes there. What happened was farcical. All the Haida who had the wherewithal had departed for Sitka, expecting the worst. One Indian was seized on suspicion but he managed to wrench himself free and dove overboard, leaving his blanket behind. Chief Weah, who was on board, followed suit. And then, to make the ship's officers feel even better about things, the man who had made his getaway by diving overboard returned in a canoe and harangued the ship long and loud. Up to now, he cried, he had trusted the white man, but now that they'd taken to stealing a poor man's blanket—well, what was the world coming to? "With wonderful forbearance," wrote one officer, "we submitted to his abuse."

Edenshaw's people blamed Weah's; Weah, as should have been expected, blamed Edenshaw and his men. Edenshaw, sometimes considered the leading Haida chief of the 19th century, charmed the British officers. No one was deceived, but proving guilt beyond reasonable doubt was impossible. As the *Virago* departed, having done nothing, the people at Masset fired several of their cannon in a salute.

Later that day, somewhere near Kung, the *Virago*'s crew opened up on a foraging black bear with one of the ship's guns. After enjoying the unexpected attention for a few minutes the bear loped off to keep an appointment elsewhere. Disgusted, one Dr. Kennedy went ashore with a rifle, but he could not hit the bear either. Having roundly impressed the watching Haida, the crew of the *Virago* discovered the ship was dragging anchor and almost on the rocks.

While sounding the western entrance to Houston Stewart Channel two days later, two of the *Virago*'s boats were attacked by pirates from Ninstints on Anthony Island. All that saved the crewmen was a breeze that allowed the boats to outsail the canoes. Again the *Virago* did nothing in retaliation, for the captain apparently believed the Haida alibi: "We thought you were people from another village." It was an age-old excuse: from the very beginning the Haida had confused whites with other Haida, or protested their innocence while blaming another village. It worked with the captain of the *Virago* just as well as it had worked 60 and 70 years earlier with the maritime fur traders.

But sometimes the pirates were caught in the act by men who probably knew the Haida as well as the Haida did themselves. Men, for instance, like Captain William McNeill, who, after a lifetime spent on the coast, would die in his own bed in his own farmhouse in Oak Bay, then a farming community outside Victoria. As the master of the *Beaver* in August 1854 he discovered the brigantine *Vancouver* wrecked on Rose Spit. This was the second HBC ship by that name to hit the sandspit, and like the earlier *Vancouver*, the Haida were "salvaging" whatever was loose, even before the ship was abandoned. McNeill stood by watching Captain Reid do exactly what was expected of him in the circumstances, knowing full well that if he did not, McNeill would. In his report McNeill was brief—and blunt.

"I must mention that after all had been done possible to save the *Vancouver*, Captain Reid set fire to her, as he says she was breaking up and the sea making a complete breach over her. The Indians had begun to plunder and break up the vessel. Those Massets again, as it was they gave some annoyance. It is now time that this Edenso [Edenshaw] and his gang were punished." [15]

At this point the black cloth is again dropped over the islands. The HBC continued to trade on the islands, just as the Haida continued to make their trips to Fort Simpson and southern points. Nothing further is known of events until 1858 and 1859, when American miners, attracted to the Fraser River and disappointed with what they found there, continued north to the islands to renew the now almost decade-old search for gold.

According to one writer, two of these miners, identified only as Charlie Blake and Barney Goldsworthy, prospectors working out of Victoria, were captured by the Haida and spent two years on the islands as slaves. Inadvertently their predicament was discovered and reported to Fort Victoria by Billy Pottinger, a Scotsman who worked as a scout and messenger for John Tod, chief factor at Fort Kamloops. Later that same summer the two were ransomed for an unreported number of blankets.

None of this last wave of gold miners to the islands found anything. A few years later, the next mining expedition to the islands would not be looking for gold, and one of the miners would be successful, at least on paper.

CHAPTER SIX

VISITORS, MISSIONARIES AND GHOSTS

COPPER

IN 1862 AN expedition sent north by the HBC, and guided by Chief Edenshaw, located iron and copper deposits on the Copper Islands in Skincuttle Inlet on the east coast of Moresby Island. Interested men with money in Victoria formed the Queen Charlotte Mining Company in 1862 as a result of these discoveries. Francis Poole, an Englishman newly arrived from Canada West was hired to go north with a crew to investigate. Poole was a mining engineer, though some have doubted his qualifications; he was, as can be seen by anyone reading his book, an intelligent and cautious man, and he became the first European to live on the islands. Contrary to what was expected, Poole had virtually no trouble with the "Vikings of the North Pacific".

His peaceful time may be attributed to a number of co-existent factors: the southern Haida respected the Royal Navy, due to its actions farther south among the Kwakiutl of Vancouver Island; the Haida were involved in the whisky trade on the coast, which was centred in the Fort Simpson vicinity; once again the east-coast villages were fighting inter se wars; and Kloo, the chief of the nearby village of Tanu, had been spoken to.

Before sailing north Poole visited Governor Douglas in Victoria who "regretted that he could not take upon himself the responsibility of giving me the more substantial protection of a gunboat and a detachment of marines. The hostility attributed to the natives of Queen Charlotte Islands the Governor declared to be well founded.

Chief Albert Edward Edenshaw (right) and a younger chief, photographed by George M. Dawson, in 1878. (COURTESY GEOLOGICAL SURVEY OF CANADA)

The risk and expense would be too great, he said, for the Government to incur in a private undertaking; but he ended some valuable advice by recommending me strongly to supply myself with plenty of arms and ammunition.

"It was not very encouraging. I was bent upon making the venture, however. As it chanced, Kitguen [Kloo or Klue], who claimed the head chieftainship of the islands, was then at Victoria; so I took him before the Governor, to whom he promised that his tribe should not molest us, and that he would bring his influence or power to bear in our behalf should any other tribe seem disposed to contest our landing or interfere with our explorations." [1]

Poole reached Skincuttle Inlet on August 11, 1862 and departed April 6, 1864. Although he left no mark on the islands except for some mine shafts on Skincuttle and Burnaby islands, neither of which revealed anything worth the effort, the account he wrote of his stay records the third turning point in the 19th-century Haida history of the Queen Charlotte Islands.

SMALLPOX

In October 1863 "an outbreak of the small-pox among the Indians brought things to a head," wrote Poole. "Several died, one of whom

101

was a handy fellow, called 'Indian George' by my men, and another, a pretty little girl. Seeing these two were dying, the Indians strangled them, and immediately after struck their filthy camp on Skincuttle, making off in a body, and leaving us to bury their dead, if we chose to perform that office. This we did, to prevent the further spread of the small-pox."

Two months later, on his way back to the islands from the northern mainland, Poole brought with him a white man who was trying to make his way back to Victoria. "As ill-luck would have it, what should he do but fall sick of small-pox," and the skipper of the vessel refused to carry the man farther than Poole's camp. "We whites," Poole explained later, "were not attacked; but scarce had the sick man landed when the Indians again caught it; and in a very short space of time some of our best friends of the Ninstence [Ninstints] or Cape St. James tribe...had disappeared for ever from the scene. It was long before health could be restored to the surroundings of our little colony." [2]

Smallpox was new to the people of the Queen Charlotte Islands. Signs of the disease had been noted among the Kaigani Haida of Alaska half a century earlier, and it is thought that the infected had caught smallpox at Sitka. Nothing in the written or oral records suggests that the Queen Charlotte Islands were affected to any extent by the epidemics sweeping up and down the Northwest Coast from the 1740s into the late 1850s. Isolated cases of smallpox, or people scarred by the disease, were noticed, but in at least one case this "evidence" is from Alaska, where smallpox raged in the epidemic of 1836. Until the 1840s the islands' relative isolation was a blessing. However, by the 1850s this buffer had begun to shrink drastically: Europeans were travelling about the islands in increasing numbers, and the Haida who could get off the islands were spending much of the year at Fort Victoria and points farther south. It was only a matter of time until the inevitable happened.

The epidemic that hit the islanders started in Victoria and can be dated to March 13, 1862. Smallpox reached the Indian camping grounds around the Inner Harbour within a month and began to spread quickly. This was due largely to the crowded conditions, the lack of sanitation, and the authorities' initial disregard. When it realized the enormity of what was happening, Governor Douglas's government at first isolated these people and restricted the movement of more Indians into the area. That did no one any good; so, as if to brush the problem away, its next step was to force the coast Indians—Kwakiutl, Tsimshian and Tlingit—probably several thousand in number, to return home. Thus smallpox spread up the coast.

Hundreds died attempting to reach home, and hundreds more were infected when the first survivors reached their villages. One group of Haida making its way north was attacked and wiped out by a party of Kwakiutl. In turn, these people were infected and carried smallpox home with them. No one bothered to collect the stories of the survivors, largely because no one cared. Among the first people to see the results of this epidemic were American and British travellers, explorers and missionaries. Without exception these people saw exactly what they expected to see. None of them realized what had happened: some because they had not known the Haida prior to 1862, some because they were so horrified by what had taken place that they wiped it from their memories; others, who expected to see wild and degenerate Indians, saw them; and then came the missionaries whose actions and words frequently implied that, had the Indians known of Christianity and been good Christians in those days, everyone would still be alive.

Though the story of the islands is lacking in detail, during the late 1850s and most of the 1860s, the outline is etched in black. According to some experts, there were as many as 10,000 Haida living in the islands in 1774 when Perez tried to find a safe anchorage off Langara Island. John Work made a rough head count of the people living in the 13 Haida villages in 1841, and decided there were 6,693 people on the islands. Robert Brown, a Scottish naturalist who visited the islands briefly in 1866, thought Work's estimate low and suggested there had been some 10,000 Haida on the islands in 1841. "Since that period," Brown wrote, "intestine and foreign war, disease, debauchery, and general decay, have decimated their number. I do not suppose that, at the present day, there are more than 5,000 Hydahs, all told, and not more than 3,000 permanently, or at one time, resident on the islands." [3] Another, more recent, estimate of the population claims there was a pre-epidemic population of 9,618; this had diminished to 1,658 by 1870. Even though these figures include the Alaska Haida, the pall of death must have hung like smoke over the islands.

These final figures state that 83% of the Haida died. Yet almost nothing is said of all this; one island historian almost ignores the disease and what it did, and some of the best historians to write about the Northwest Coast imply—by their lack of interest or concern—that losing more than three-quarters of their population was no more important to the Haida than the problems caused by alcohol, and the social unrest arising from European contact and a rapidly changing way of life. Ironically, no sooner had smallpox and other diseases killed three out of every four people on the Queen Charlotte Islands, than the outside world began to show some interest in the world of the Haida.

NEW VIEWS

Robert Brown was one of the first of these interested visitors. In his day Vancouver Island had at last begun to be developed by colonists. The mainland colony of British Columbia was growing, as gold continued to lure hundreds of miners and merchants into the still largely unknown interior. Realizing that his readers might be interested in the future development of the islands, Brown discussed the possible settlement of the Queen Charlottes.

Brown was not a man with many illusions. "The soil is poor," he wrote, "and the country being thickly wooded, I do not think that, even under the most favourable circumstances, it will ever be worth settling on for agricultural purposes. The climate is so wet that, though wheat and other cereals might be cultivated, crops would be very precarious." He thought that as long as there was land on the mainland and Vancouver Island, the islands would remain the home of the Haida. "In one sentence," he concluded, "these islands are more interesting to the geographer than to the colonist; to the miner they may be valuable, but to the agriculturist they are useless." [4]

James Swan, an American living at Port Townsend, wrote about the islands in 1873. "These Islands form together a healthy picturesque territory, rich in natural resources, and well adapted to colonization. Nevertheless, for the space of nearly a century no attempt has been made by the English to colonize them. There they lie waste and fallow, yet marvellously productive, and awaiting nothing but capital, enterprise, and skill to return manifold profit to those who will develop their resources."

It is a nice piece of work, but it was based on what the Haida visiting Port Townsend told him, not what he saw for himself. He did see their canoes and these were "very large and capable of carrying one hundred persons with all their equipment for a long voyage. But those generally used will carry from twenty to thirty persons; and in these conveyances they make voyages of several hundred miles." Striking as these canoes were, he did not think them as graceful as those made by people on the west coast of Washington Territory and Vancouver Island.

"The Haidas," that Swan encountered at Port Townsend, brought with them "as articles of traffic, furs of various kinds, dogfish, and seal oil, and carvings in wood and stone, as well as ornaments in silver of excellent workmanship, such as bracelets, finger-rings, and ear ornaments.

"A peculiar kind of slate-stone [argillite] is found on Queen Charlotte's Islands, very soft when first quarried, and easily carved into fanciful figures of various kinds, but growing very hard upon exposure to the air, and after being rubbed with oil, which seems to harden and polish it.

"These stone carvings are eagerly purchased by persons looking for Indian curiosities, and are generally regarded by casual observers as idols, or objects of worship, or indicative in some manner of their secret or mystic rites. This, however, is an error. None of the tribes of the northwest coast worship idols or any visible symbol of their secret religion, which is confined to the totem, or tamananawis, or guardian spirit of each individual Indian." [5]

Lady Dufferin went ashore at Skidegate on September 1, 1876, while her husband hunted bear in the vicinity. Accompanied by her travelling companions, she "went to a little trading settlement, where an American is buying oil. The Indians were in tents and lying about the shore; the day was lovely and warm, and we had great fun bargaining, buying silver bracelets and carved bowls." Back on board she was amused to watch the buying and selling going on, furs and bracelets, old clothes, soap, tobacco, and biscuits being exchanged, while "hideous faces, painted black or red, looked up from the canoes." [6]

Few of these people more than mention smallpox. Molyneux St. John, who accompanied Lord and Lady Dufferin on their trip to the Queen Charlotte Islands, seems to have had more than a passing knowledge of the Haida, but appears ignorant of the result of the smallpox epidemic only years earlier. The closest he comes to realizing something had occurred was this observation. During "the last few years a great change has taken place in the once fierce and intractable Hydahs, and [it] unfortunately by no means resembles the change that, to a greater or lesser extent, is working among the Tsimpseans [of Metlakatla, William Duncan's world-famous village of Christian Indians]."

Unhappily he could not leave it at that, but had to go on and repeat what many in Victoria were saying. "The early visits of the...Islanders to Victoria gave them a taste for the debauchery of civilization....They have abandoned their predatory excursions, and now, taking their young women with them they set out for Victoria, timing their visit to be there during the season when the miners are arriving from the interior. During their stay in their own homes, much of their time is spent in carving bone, slate, or silver ornaments...for sale in Victoria. They have become lazy and will not work, while at the same time their greed for money is intense, so that even the virtue of their families has ceased to be respected by them, and their homes have become nurseries for the streets of Victoria." [7]

CARVING

It was a black time for the Haida, yet, if Marius Barbeau was right when he maintained that the Haida did not carve any significant poles before the 1840s or '50s, then most of the major stands of totems were being raised at this time—from the money earned by supposedly nefarious activities in Victoria, according to some. So few are the recorded details regarding this creative burst, no one can know for sure what took place.

Along with the increasingly large number of totems that were being raised, argillite carving began to flourish about this same time. Although the first such carvings had begun to appear about 1818 or so, it was not until the gold rush made a town out of sleepy Fort Victoria that the carvers found a steady market for this art work. By the 1870s the tourist trade had begun to open up the coast, and the Haida carvers no longer had to make the trip to Victoria. They could sell their work just as easily in trading posts at Fort Simpson and Sitka.

No matter who the carver was, and what his outward reasons were for carving, all the Haida carvers of this period must have been united by one central theme. "Carving was also a means of escaping the trauma of change, a way of recapturing the past that seemed to be fading rapidly." [8]

ABANDONED VILLAGES

Reverend Collison, one of the first half-dozen Europeans to live on the islands, and the second to write a book about life there, rarely mentions the ravages of the 1862-63 smallpox epidemic—and he arrived only 13 years later. To do him justice, Collison does quote one man's speech, a response to Collison's first sermon at Masset.

"Our people are brave in warfare and never turn their backs on their foes, but this foe we could not see and we could not fight. Our medicine men are wise, but they could not drive away the evil spirit, and why? Because it was the sickness of the Iron People [Europeans]. It came from them. You have visited our camps, and you have seen many of the lodges empty. In them the campfires once burned brightly, and around them the hunters and warriors told of their deeds in the past. Now the fires have gone out and the brave men have fallen before the Iron Man's sickness. You have come too late for them." [9]

The camps were indeed empty. Of the Haida towns on Moresby Island and nearby islands, Chaatl, Kaisun, Ninstints, Tanu, Skedans, Kunhalas and Cumshewa were abandoned by the 1870s, though some were used as camps into the 20th century. Much the same is true of all but two of the towns on or near Graham Island. Haina, largely populated by families from Kaisun and Chaatl, lost much of its population to Skidegate in the 1880s. Kayang was in the process of being abandoned in 1884. Those left at Yan moved to Masset sometime around 1890. When George Dawson visited Hiellen in 1878 it was a ghost town, as were Kung and Kiusta. And Dadens may have been abandoned as early as 1800, its residents moving to join relatives in Alaska after a fire levelled the town. Yaku, only a mile and a half from Kiusta, of which Yaku is sometimes considered a part, was deserted by the 1890s. Tian—Slaughter Village—on the

Ruins of communal house at Kung, 1906. (FROM SHELDON, 1912)

west coast of Graham Island and one of the really mysterious Haida villages, was abandoned by the 1850s.

Smallpox was not the cause of places like Tian being deserted, but smallpox, followed by measles and other European diseases that visitors to Victoria and Port Townsend were bringing home, does largely account for most of the other villages being left to the ghosts of better days. Life in large and virtually empty villages was untenable; at the urging of the missionaries—the Methodists at Skidegate and the Anglicans at Masset—the survivors moved to the new centres. The only trading posts on the islands were at these centres; and within a few years schools and medical help were other attractions, as was the money to be made by supplying dogfish to the oil works at Skidegate. By the 1890s, if not earlier, the only winter villages on the islands were Masset and Skidegate on Graham Island. It was in these centres, both ancient towns in their own right, that the Haida regrouped and prepared to meet the future—whatever that would mean.

Disease and Europeanization had made one thing clear to even the most doubtful and tradition-bound Haida: by the 1870s their days as the "Vikings of the North Pacific" and "piratical head-hunting Haida" were past. Some of the men lost themselves in carving, looking for a way back into the past, or looking at the past so as to be able to understand the present. Others drank. A large number of Haida probably led contented, day-to-day lives, untouched by the reality around them. How many of the women who went south and returned is unknown, but it would have been odd if many did not remain at Fort Victoria or other southern points because of men—or because of a man, as in the case of Captain Pickett's wife. But of all the ways the Haida found to deal with the traumatic changes in the islands, one man's response caught everyone by surprise.

Gedanst, a youngster from one of the leading Eagle families in the islands, became a practising Christian. This took place in Victoria about 1866. Gedanst, who became Amos Russ (named in honour of a little-known Methodist missionary), had lived an enviable life in Skidegate. When he was still only a child his maternal grandfather, one of the leading chiefs at Skidegate, decided the boy would one day take his place. He was, it was said, "a youth of great promise and bravery, an initiate of one of the dancing societies and therefore convinced, as were his fellow Indians, that his vigils, fasts, ordeals and solitary communings in the forest had earned him occult powers and the approval of his guardian spirit."

Christianity changed all this. In 1875 Gedanst asked William Collison, then based at Fort Simpson, to move to Skidegate, but Collison was unable to, having already promised to go to Masset. It was said that the young Christian cut down his family totems to prove to his grandfather that he was going to remain a Christian. "I want to help our people," he was reported to have said, "to be strong, in the same way that the white man is strong." [10]

BUSINESS

Another equally radical change took place on the islands at about this same time. "An enterprising American [Charley the Langleyman] anxious to open trade with the Haida for their fur-seal and sea otter skins, arrived there on a sloop with a cargo of goods. Having secured the protection and support of one of the chiefs by a number of gifts, he succeeded in erecting a strong blockhouse. Here he landed and stored his goods. He had brought with him also a quantity of liquor and firearms and a small brass cannon. The latter would seem to be the necessary accompaniment of the former.

"The cannon he kept loaded, and placed in a position commanding the approach to the door. Yet all his precautions proved inefficient. One dark night the Indians surrounded the house and proceeded to fire into it, so that, in order to save his life, having first barricaded the entrance, he escaped through an opening in the rear under cover of the darkness and fled to Skidegate, a distance of over a hundred miles, where he hired a canoe and crew of Indians to convey him to Fort Simpson."

There, Collison continues, Charley the Langleyman offered what remained of his house and stock to the Hudson's Bay Company, which had been looking for a foothold on the islands. The company paid him a small sum for it, but its difficulty was to find a man to take charge. A trader by the name of Rutland at Metlakatla was the HBC's first choice, but he did not accept the posting. The man who took his place was one A. Cooper, who remained at Masset from 1871 to 1874.

"At length," Collison writes, apparently unaware of Cooper's time at Masset, "a man was found whose Indian wife, a Tsimshian, was known to the Haida, and who guaranteed his safety should she accompany him. Her promise had been fulfilled; she informed me that she had on several occasions saved him from their hands when they would have killed him."

The man was Martin Offut. Collison described him as a man who "had travelled across the American continent about the time of the great Mormon massacre [possibly a reference to the so-called "Mormon War" of the 1850s]; had owned all the land on which Sacramento now stands, and had kept a saloon there during the California gold excitement. There he had amassed fortunes, and had squandered them again, and at length had drifted up the coast to prospect for gold in Alaska. Now that he had settled down among the Indians, he had become as one of them. He attended their potlatches, received and carried away what was given to him, and, when his wife or daughter was ill, he called in the medicine sorcerers, and paid them for performing their incantations over the patient." [11]

In short, Offut was the perfect man for the HBC job at Masset in 1874. And if the Indians had tried to kill him, as they had his predecessor, it was not due to their "piratical head-hunting" proclivities; it was because the chiefs were tired of what alcohol was doing to their people now that it was right in front of them and available for a pittance. Most of the time, though, Offut was doing things right, for he survived and returned to Fort Simpson, hale and hearty, in 1878. Alexander McKenzie, who became the islands' first justice of the peace, replaced Offut. Other managers followed until the HBC closed the store on June 1, 1898.

During the last decades of the 19th century the HBC were not the only people doing business on the islands. From 1868 or so to the mid-1870s, McKay and Spring, a firm already operating a trading post in Kyuquot Sound, Vancouver Island, opened a small post near Cumshewa at a place now called McCoy Cove. McKay and Spring were among the first independent fur traders based in what would soon become British Columbia, for they had started out running a saltery and cooperage at Sooke. They were also one of the first international companies on the coast: by 1868 they were operating the *Favorite* in the freighting business between Victoria and the Hawaiian Islands, as well as points between Acapulco and Sitka. By 1873 the *Favorite* was in the sealing business and in at least one subsequent year she went out with a crew of Haida hunters. It was not a successful trip. Being devout Christians by this time, the Haida would not hunt on Sundays.

The Church Missionary Society Arrives

While this activity was developing on the islands, a new face had appeared at Fort Simpson. This was William Collison, but the story behind his arrival began two decades earlier and was largely the result of the *Virago*'s time in the area. Her captain, James Prevost, a religious man, had returned to England from duty on the west coast and pleaded with the Church Missionary Society to send missionaries out to the British portion of the Northwest Coast. This they did, and William Duncan arrived in October 1857. Probably one of the most important men on the coast during his lifetime, and certainly one of the few really successful missionaries, Duncan resolved to move his people away from the whisky traders and other distracting white influences at Fort Simpson. In 1862 he founded the Christian village of Metlakatla. Other missionaries were sent out to help Duncan, but he was not an easy man to work with, so they drifted away, some to go into business, others to return to England. In November 1873 William Henry Collison and his wife, Marion, arrived from England. They would stay.

The next year Collison, who would go on to become Archdeacon of New Caledonia, met "a fine young [Haida] chief named Seegay," and as Seegay's wife spoke both Tsimshian and Haida, Collison, who could speak Tsimshian, was able to carry on a conversation with the chief. The next year when the Haida fleet returned to Metlakatla to sell canoes and potatoes, and whatever else they had managed to scrape together, Collison was able to renew his acquaintance with Seegay and his wife, and again did his best in the time available "to teach them the way of Life and Salvation". In 1876 Seegay's wife appealed to Collison to visit the islands and talk with Seegay, who was dying from the effects of exposure as the result of a canoe accident. Collison did what he could for Seegay, preached to the Haida at Masset—a congregation of doubters that included Edenshaw, who had the notion that people who "embraced Christianity" freed their slaves—and decided to return to open a mission at the first opportunity.

This he did. Collison and his family arrived at Masset aboard the HBC's *Otter* early in November 1876. His mission was a success, almost from the start. Accompanied by his wife and his two small sons, one of whom was the first white child born at Metlakatla, he plunged into the daily life of the Haida. His Christianity was, like Duncan's, as much a social as a religious programme, and Collison was not afraid of the Haida. Nor was his wife. Marion Collison was a deaconess, had served as a nurse on the battlefields of the Franco-Prussian War, and was in Metz when that city surrendered to the Germans in 1870. The Collisons' daughter, Emily, was the first white child born on the islands.

One measure of Collison's success was that within two years of the opening of his school at Masset in 1876, the government made money

The Collisons' mission at Masset, 1878. (COURTESY GEOLOGICAL SURVEY OF CANADA)

available to him for education and medical care. Collison fought the influence of the shamans successfully, and encouraged the people to clean up their village; eventually they began building European-style houses. Also he was the vehement enemy of gambling and drinking.

On the less doctrinaire side, Collison seems to have managed to talk Offut into marrying his Tsimshian wife; either that or the happy-go-lucky Offut, whom Collison had begun to refer to as "the squire", decided to marry his lady knowing how it would please Reverend Collison.

Collison's stay on the islands lasted until November 1879, when he returned to Metlakatla to take charge of affairs there. He was replaced by George Sneath, a young man who left little trace of his two years at Masset. Sneath was replaced by Charles Harrison, who would leave an unexpectedly large mark on the islands.

Harrison and his wife were liked by the Haida and he seems to have been an energetic preacher. However, he had a drinking problem and was ill much of the time; this ill health was thought by some to be nothing more than laziness and lack of direction. At one point he accidentally burned the mission house to the ground, at another he became a storekeeper. By late 1888 even his relationship with the Haida had turned sour, and he begged Collison to pay a visit to Masset and smooth out the problems. By 1890 Harrison was back in England and in August of that year John H. Keen and his wife replaced the Harrisons.

An even worse problem than any of the above troubles came to haunt Harrison. In the correspondence later gathered together by the Church Missionary Society, there are hints suggesting Harrison's difficulties were far more complex than the public knew. Today the only explanation that works with all the facts is that the Harrisons' first child, a boy, was half Haida.

After he was forced to resign from the CMS, Harrison and his family, of all things, returned to the islands as settlers. He farmed, became one of the islands' biggest promoters, preached whenever there was a chance, and was appreciated by everyone. It was at this time that he wrote a series of articles for an island newspaper that he later rewrote and published as *Ancient Warriors of the North Pacific*. It is a study of the Haida and the islands that, while never boring, can never be fully trusted.

Alexander McKenzie, who bought property on Delkatla Slough at Masset shortly after he quit managing the HBC store in 1887, became the islands' first settler. McKenzie had fallen in love with the islands.

VISITORS FOR BETTER OR WORSE

George Dawson was the first Canadian scientist to reach the islands. He spent the summer of 1878 exploring the north and east coasts of the islands, as well as Skidegate Channel. Although Dawson's *Report on the Queen Charlotte Islands*, published in 1880, was the third book of consequence about the islands to appear (the first and second being Beresford's *A Voyage Around the World* and Poole's *Queen Charlotte Islands*) it was the first Canadian book about the place.

Dawson was the last writer to visit all the villages while the majority of them were still inhabited and in many cases his comments and photographs are virtually the only record of these places. About the same time Dawson, a gifted writer, published an intelligent and sympathetic piece about the Haida in *Harper's Monthly Magazine*.

At Masset Dawson wrote, "The village just mentioned is called *Ut-te-was*, and here is situated a Hudson's Bay post—the only one on the Islands—and a station of the Church Missionary Society, in charge at the time of our visit, in August, 1878, of Rev. Mr. Collison....About a mile south of this place, also on the east shore, is a second village, and on the opposite side a third. Though all these are now decaying and with comparatively few inhabitants, Masset must at one time have been a very populous place."

George Mercer Dawson. (COURTESY CHARLES LILLARD)

At another place Dawson states that near Skidegate, "In the cove at Imate Point some rude buildings have been erected in connection with the dog-fish fishery, in which two persons were engaged at the time of our visit. Half a mile inland a few trees have been felled for the purpose of obtaining wood for barrels, and a little opening made which enables one to form some idea of the straightness and size of the trees composing the forest." [12] Details like this do not exist anywhere else. William Sterling and J. Mc.B Smith, the two men Dawson mentioned, had been working in their cove since 1876. Smith told Dawson he thought some 250 people lived at Skidegate when they were not in Victoria.

A few years after Dawson's visit, the Canadian government, which had long ignored the Haida and their deteriorating situation, decided that the land on the islands must be set aside for the use of Europeans. In 1882 Peter O'Reilly, the Indian Reserve Commissioner, staked out the first Haida reserves on the Queen Charlotte Islands. His report is straightforward, even icy in the face of the thousands of Haida who had died since 1862.

"At Masset," O'Reilly wrote, "I commenced my work, having first had an interview with the principal chief, 'Wee-ah' and a few of his people, the greater portion of the tribe being absent engaged in fishing. I fully explained the object of my mission and the desire of the Dominion Government to see his people advance in civilization and living more like their white brethren; to which he replied that they had long expected me, and were glad that at last their lands were to be secured for them."

As a result, Weah, perhaps the greatest of the late 19th-century chiefs, was reduced to being chief of something like 770 acres of land. Hiellen, an ancient village site and once a large town, was reduced to a 75-acre plot.

"Yan, the second village of importance on the northern portion of these islands, occupies an exposed position at the western entrance to Masset Inlet; it is presided over by a sub-chief named 'Na-thlung'. I have here reserved 300 acres, which includes a long strip of land on the sea coast, formerly cultivated as potato gardens. The soil is light and sandy, and would not stand continuous cropping. Good timber is scarce, owing to forest fires having swept this part of the country some few years back, there is enough, however, for the purpose of fuel."

Of the 16 reserves set aside by O'Reilly on the northern shores of Graham Island, only Masset and Yatze were inhabited. The latter town was a relatively new place and would soon be abandoned. That left Masset. The people of Skidegate and the southern portion of the islands fared no better.

Skidegate became a 900-acre reserve, bounded at the southern end by the Skidegate Oil Company. Cumshewa was reduced to an 80-

Haidas at Yatze, 1878. (COURTESY GEOLOGICAL SURVEY OF CANADA)

115

acre reserve and described as "having once been a large village," but was then a village of 30 and the site was "utterly worthless except as a halibut fishery". There is a note of sadness in his final words about the place, "In all probability this band will remove to Skidegate within a few years, and add another band to the long list of deserted villages on this coast."

At the time of O'Reilly's visit, Skedans had only a population of 25 people, who told him they were moving to Skidegate, and the village was a wreck. "The reserve is very worthless, being almost entirely rocky, mountain land, covered with timber. About four acres have once been cultivated as potato patches, which is all that is available for the purpose; it is, however, a good halibut and herring fishing station."

Between 30 and 50 people lived at Tanu, a reserve of 65 acres on Tanu Island. The land was heavily wooded, but otherwise worthless in O'Reilly's opinion. The people there did not impress him, as "these Indians have, within the last 20 years, so degenerated that it is hard to realize that they ever were a powerful tribe." [13] There is no mention of smallpox in his report.

Uninterested as O'Reilly was, the man did report what he saw and thought. James Swan, who visited the islands in 1883, kept much of what he saw to himself. So far as Swan was concerned the Haida were still a remote and mysterious people.

When he reached the islands ten years after his first foray into Haida anthropology and history, he was known the length of the Northwest Coast as a writer, homesteader, businessman, and judge. He was also, among other things, a busy and enthusiastic collector for the Smithsonian Institution. A passage from the report of his second trip sums up the changes in island life.

"At the village of Laskeek, on Tanoo [Tanu] Island, is the most interesting collection of columns, both heraldic and mortuary, and more monuments for the dead than I had seen in any other village. The Indian house in which I stopped is a new one, of large dimensions, built after the ancient style. In this house will be held the most extensive ceremonies that have taken place for many years, consisting of the tomanawas or secret performances, then the public tattooing of persons of all ages and sexes, then the masquerade dances and the distribution of presents, when several thousand dollars' worth of blankets, calico, clothing, and provisions will be given away, and the whole interspersed with feasts at different houses in the village. The occasion of this is the erection of one or more huge columns, elaborately carved with totemic devices, to show the wealth and importance of the chief in front of whose house the column will be erected.

"This great ceremony will take place in the fall of this year and will be well worth seeing, as it is probable that it will be the last grand display of the kind that will take place, the influence of missionaries being directed to suppressing these ancient ceremonies, in which they have succeeded, so far as regards the villages at Masset and Skidegate, where the ceremonies of the tomanawas, if performed at present, are greatly shorn of their honors, and I was thereby enabled to obtain many articles of ceremonial usage, which formerly no white man was suffered to look at, much less to purchase and take away."

In two paragraphs Swan sums up the passing of an ancient way of life. The size of the potlatch, which would soon lead to the Canadian government's prohibiting further potlatches, was, like the raising of totems, pure ostentation. European visitors were blaming missionaries for trying to maintain some sort of control over a society both out of sync and hell bent on suicide, while never acknowledging—perhaps never realizing—the damage disease and alcohol were doing to the islanders. By 1883 the explorer was sometimes a scientist, sometimes an amateur, but always a collector. Such themes would echo in the island for a century.

In one final paragraph, Swan outlined his activities: "The result of my work may be briefly summed up as follows: I have a most interesting and valuable collection of articles of Indian manufacture. I have succeeded in introducing the black cod, a new and valuable food-fish. I have determined the locality of several new inlets and harbors on the west coast of Graham Island. I have succeeded in deciphering the true meaning of the hieroglyphics of the carved columns, which are in great profusion in every village, and the meaning of the tattoo marks on the persons of the natives. I have collected evidence of the former intercourse between the Haidahs and the Aztec races of Mexico, and have accumulated an amount of information respecting the interesting tribe inhabiting the Queen Charlotte group of islands never yet made public, but which I shall elaborate for publication." [14]

Newton H. Chittenden, an American writer, lawyer and traveller, reached the Queen Charlotte Islands in 1884 as an agent for the Honourable William Smithe, Chief Commissioner of Lands and Works of the Province of British Columbia. Although he wrote as an explorer, Chittenden was reporting on the country he saw with respect to settlement. "Owing to their isolated position...they are at the present time practically unexplored and unknown. But the advancing tide of emigration is now setting far up the north coast and will soon invade the home of the Hydahs."

Although his published report lacks the geographical and anthropological value of Dawson's, Chittenden's offers more general details. "There are three villages near the entrance to Massett Inlet: Yan—abandoned—with 20 houses and 25 carved poles, on the west side, and Utte-was—now Massett—and Ka-Yung, situated about a mile below, on the east. Massett is the principal village of the Hyda nation, now containing a population of about three hundred and fifty Indians, 40 occupied houses, 50 carved poles, and the ruins of many ancient lodges." Skidegate is an "imposing village, finely situated, containing 30 houses and 55 carved poles. A Methodist Mission, Church, and School building occupies a prominent site in the background."

Chittenden could also provide local colour. "The waters of Skidegate Inlet, during the months of June and July, were alive with canoe-loads of men, women and children, plying between the dog-fishing grounds, their villages and the works of the Skidegate Oil Company. The latter are situated on Sterling Bay, a beautiful little harbor on the north shore of the inlet, about three miles from Skidegate. Here, as previously stated, were assembled at times a numerous fleet of canoes and hundreds of natives from all parts of the island, with their klootchmen [women], papooses and dogs. The latter gave us a series of concerts which will never be forgotten.

"Nin-Ging-Wash, the ranking chief of Skidegate, is about 65 years old, thick-set, broad-faced, with a grave expression and quiet, reserved manner. He was introduced to me as the richest Indian on the island, as having the best houses, finest canoes and youngest wife. A few years ago he gave away his second wife—growing old—and sued for the daughter of Scotsgu, the leading chieftain of the west coast. Presently she made her appearance, a sprightly young woman about 26 years old, and we all started in their canoe for their home at Skidegate, where I had been invited.

"En route, while passing a pipe from the chief to his wife, my oar caught in the water, giving the canoe a sudden lurch, which would have been quite alarming to most feminine nerves, but not the princess, for she laughed so heartily over the mishap that I saw a smile spread over the big face of the old chief. An hour brought us to the broad sandy beach of Skidegate, opposite the chief's present residence, a plain, comfortable frame house, in the center of the village. Two large, splendid canoes were carefully housed in front. A small orchard, in which a few half-grown apples were seen, next engaged the attention. The chief's wife carried the keys to the house and to the piles of trunks and boxes it contained. Their furniture embraced good modern beds, tables, dressing cases, mirrors, chairs, stove, lamps and other articles too numerous to mention.

"They opened trunk after trunk and box after box, and showed me a very interesting collection of Indian wear; four masquerade head dresses, reaching down to the waist, covered with ermine skins, valued at $30 each; several complete dancing suits, including a beautiful one made by the princess; Indian blankets, woven by hand from the wool of the mountain sheep; masks, rattles, etc., and also a good supply of common blankets and other stores, which they exhibited with evident pride. We next ransacked their old house, a large one, still in good repair, which stood a few rods distant. Fourteen copper towers [coppers] of various sizes, formerly valued at from $50 to $500 each, leaned against the broad front. The carved pole [before the house] is so tall that when erected Nin-Ging-Wash received his present name, which signifies 'the long stick.' The house was filled with articles of Indian manufacture, curiously carved cooking and eating utensils, fishing implements, boxes, mats, etc. The chief's property, real and personal, is worth several thousand dollars." [15]

What seems like Chittenden's excessive interest in Nin-Ging-Wash's personal inventory was not a quirk. Swan had been equally interested, and for the same reason. By the mid-1870s collectors, both private and public, were willing to spend a good deal of money on Northwest Coast artifacts. By the time it was all over, "the city of Washington contained more Northwest Coast material than the state of Washington, and New York City probably housed more British Columbia material than did British Columbia." [16] One reason for the British Columbia situation was that Frank Kermode, director of the British Columbia Provincial Museum, had little interest in local anthropology and history.

A British Columbian who was interested was Dr. Charles F. Newcombe and he became one of BC's best-known collectors. An Englishman with brief but successful careers as both alienist and general practitioner in England and the United States, Newcombe came to Victoria for his wife's health. After her death and his own inability to establish himself professionally, he lost his heart to the Queen Charlotte Islands, about which he was undoubtedly the ultimate authority during the 1890s. But love of islands and their people will not feed a growing family, so he began collecting what is usually termed Haida "artifacts," but actually included anything that was loose—from old bones to entire houses.

"Collector" is the term used here, and men like Newcombe were, in one sense, specialists hired by museums to fill orders, but some of this work was so mundane and required so little expertise, that "middleman" might be a better description of them. Money aside, this task consumed so much of Newcombe's time that he never published an iota of what he knew about the Haida and the Queen Charlotte Islands. That this is regrettable can be seen in "Notes of a Journey Round the Southern Islands of the Queen Charlotte Group," a manuscript he never got around to publishing. The trip took place in 1901; Newcombe was accompanied by Henry Moody, and much of the Haida information was obtained from Tom Price, chief of Ninstints.

The 20th century would give a good deal for more information like this: "Passing a point, Lokalas, on the north side, about three quarters of a mile beyond it, the old village is seen, Gaisun, on the north side of the harbor, with a small stream dividing it into two nearly equal parts. About the year 1840...there were reported to be eighteen houses here, and 320 inhabitants. It must have been soon after this time that this village lost all its fighting men when returning home from a raid after slaves into the Kwakiutl country. Old men still relate that when they were boys, three or four canoes from Gaisun were waylaid by Tsimshians at Lasxail, a place with a small fort, near the south end of Banks Island, and not one man ever returned. They never recovered from this blow.

"Two houses are still standing and fifteen carved poles of which only one is a xat or mortuary pole. In it repose the remains of the wife of the Gaisun chief. She was the first to find gold in British Columbia, and her discovery led to a rush of prospectors in 1852....The cross board of the mortuary pole bears the moon crest. With the house poles the beaver is particularly common as the lowest figure and the eagle as an upper crest."

Elsewhere Newcombe tells us that "Ninstints village is not of very old date according to the present natives, and was inhabited by the dwindling population of the numerous villages near. Within a radius of fourteen miles from this village there were no less than thirty five permanent villages of which the names are still preserved; in addition there were eight or nine isolated forts sometimes occupied for months together, and as many camping places, in good fishing harbours or streams. Altogether, indications are very strong that this was the most thickly populated part of the Queen Charlotte

120

Islands." [17] Island history lost a good part of its story with the passing of Dr. Newcombe in 1924.

AN ARTIST ENCOUNTERS THE ISLANDS

Brown, Harrison, Swan, Newcombe—different as they were in background and professions, these men typified a restless coastal type, a type still very much in evidence a century later. They were men who loved the country, but, like a man who loved two sisters and could not decide which he loved the most, and ended up marrying neither, these men did more dreaming than talking. The books they hoped to write remained unwritten, their authority unchallenged. But even as these men were engaged in their *affaires de coeur*, a woman was engaged in a *grande passion* with the islands that would not falter until her death in 1945.

Emily Carr only visited the Queen Charlotte Islands twice, in 1912 and 1928 and then only briefly, but in her island prose sketches published in *Klee Wyck*, as well as in her evocative paintings, some of which were done as late as 1941-42, Carr touched the islands' pulse. That of the Haida, too, a people she had been aware of, if not known, from earliest childhood. The Haida had camped on various beaches within a few minutes' walk of every Victoria house in which Carr ever lived.

Perhaps no one, certainly no one in her time, has written as poetically—and sensibly—of what it was like to visit one of the islands' ghost towns. "Skedans was more open than Tanoo. The trees stood farther back from it. Behind the bay another point bit deeply into the sand, so that light came in across the water from behind the village too.

"There was no soil to be seen," Carr continued. "Above the beach it was all luxuriant growth; the earth was so full of vitality that every seed which blew across her surface germinated and burst. The growing things jumbled themselves together into a dense thicket; so tensely earnest were things about growing in Skedans that everything linked with everything else, hurrying to grow to the limit of its own capacity; weeds and weaklings alike throve in the rich moistness.

"Memories came out of this place to meet the Indians; you saw remembering in their brightening eyes and heard it in the quick hushed words they said to each other in Haida." [18] Emily Carr did not publish these thoughts for years; she knew better: British Columbia was a land of pioneers. People wanted land, they wanted their slice of the good life; no one wanted to listen to a woman who liked the landscape the way it was.

CHAPTER SEVEN

THEY CAME TO STAY

First Settler

THE FIRST man to settle on the Queen Charlotte Islands was Alexander McKenzie. This was in 1887. McKenzie had been the Hudson's Bay Company agent at Masset, since December 1878, having replaced Martin Offut, who had returned to Fort Simpson. But like many others before and since, McKenzie had lost his heart to the islands. Buying 1,015 acres along the shores of Delkatla Inlet, McKenzie settled down to making a living on the islands.

Charles Harrison bought some acreage from McKenzie and built a house near the head of the inlet, thus technically becoming the islands' second settler. The third settler was J.M.L. Alexander whose See-Watt property was near Harrison's, but on McIntyre Bay instead of on the protected shores of Delkatla Inlet. Unlike McKenzie, a single man who did little more than raise a garden on his land, and Harrison, who soon returned to England to explain himself to the Anglican authorities, Alexander was a family man with 14 dependants. Alexander planned to raise cattle, but he failed to take two things into consideration.

Although his cattle thrived on the islands, there being no natural predators, except for the occasional black bear, Alexander soon discovered that there was no market for beef. There were fewer than 500 people in and around Masset, none of whom needed fresh meat; besides, canned meat was cheaper. Alexander's second problem was the cost of transportation. Shipping beef to Skidegate and Fort

Simpson was so expensive as to be prohibitive. Even though the markets in Southeast Alaska were larger, it was equally unprofitable to ship meat north to those villages, both Haida and white. It was not long before Alexander sold what cattle he could and returned to the mainland. The cattle left behind were the ancestors of the wild cattle still to be seen in the vicinity of Masset.

Late in the 1890s, settlers began drifting in, family by family for the most part. Unlike the contemporary settlements at Cape Scott on the north end of Vancouver Island, Sointula on an island near Alert Bay, and Bella Coola on the mainland, there was no planned settlement on the islands. By 1901 there were 40 "settlers" living on the islands, mostly American and British, but how permanent they were is unknown. Seven years later 50 settlers were reported to be living in the Lawn Hill area on the east coast of Graham Island, some 12 miles north of Skidegate. A post office was opened there in April 1911. Robert Scharfee, who ran a store in the area with his wife, was the first postmaster, a position he kept until he moved to Queen Charlotte in 1923.

A post office had opened in Masset ("Massett" until 1948 when the spelling was changed, so that mail for Merritt, B.C. did not go to Massett and vice-versa) in 1910, at a time when there were at least a hundred settlers in the vicinity. The post office at Queen Charlotte

A descendant of Alexander's cattle, 1978. (COLLECTION OF CHARLES LILLARD)

had opened a year earlier in 1909, as had the office at Jedway; the post office at Tlell would open in 1912, the one at Port Clements in 1914. If post offices are any indication of white activity, Skidegate was the white centre on the islands, as its local postal service began in October 1897.

The opening of these post offices marks the start of the first surge of 20th-century migration into the Canadian west. As early as 1891, government surveyors had reported that portions of Graham Island would make good agricultural land—if drained. And to drain this land the potential settler should be independently wealthy because the job was going to be long and expensive. That people of independent means would have no reason to spend their money draining swamps when dry land—and land of proven character—was available elsewhere in British Columbia did not occur to anyone. What did occur to more than a few was that they could not help but make a profit, if they bought land for between $2.50 and five dollars an acre and sold it to the settlers who were bound to come.

BUSINESS

By 1910 the white population was estimated to be more than 3,000, and if this was an enthusiastic overestimate in 1910, it was more than correct by 1914. By that time there were schools at Masset and Skidegate, some short roads, a hospital, and a newspaper, the *Queen Charlotte News*, run by one D.R. Young. It was Young who thought Jedway, an isolated mining camp on the southeastern coast of Moresby Island, would be the metropolitan centre of the islands, while places like Skidegate and Cumshewa would be commercial cities.

Two Victoria businessmen founded the Queen Charlottes Railway Company, but even though a good deal of effort went into this project, no rails were laid. A later railway was dreamed up to run from Masset to the most important Graham Island centres, but this scheme failed to develop beyond the survey stage. Nonetheless, the dreams looked good on paper in 1913 when the government announced that several new provincial railways had been projected: the British Columbia and Alaska Railway; the British Columbia Central Railway; The Cariboo, Barkerville, and Willow River Railway; the Pacific Railway; the Prince Rupert and Port Simpson Railway; the Queen Charlotte Railway, and the Graham Island Railway.

What was happening on the islands, and what the government or writers were saying was happening, were, as happened everywhere on the BC frontier, quite different. William E. Scott, Deputy Minister of

Agriculture, visited the islands in 1913. He was not particularly impressed by what he saw on Graham Island. There were several cleared areas where truck gardens were producing vegetables and numerous types of berries, but he doubted that fruit trees could be grown for commercial purposes, despite the mild temperature. Scott estimated that it cost $300 per acre to clear land.

At Queenstown, the Graham Island Timber and Coal Company seemed to be on the brink of discovering coal. The company was also drilling for oil. The settlers were able to raise excellent potatoes, but if they had success with anything else, Scott does not mention it.

Returning to Masset, Scott next visited North Beach and predicted it would "become a popular summer resort for the residents of Prince Rupert and tourists generally". At Kliki Damen, Scott and his party turned inland to visit a settler who had drained some of the swamp or muskeg on his property and was growing potatoes. "I am of the opinion," he wrote, "that the cheapest way to handle these muskegs to any large extent would be, after thoroughly draining them, to burn off as much of the moss as possible, sow grass seed thereon, and depasture with sheep or cattle....After it had been in pasture for a few years the land probably would be sufficiently solid to plough, and could then be used for the production of crops." [1]

But few could afford to wait for a few years: few settlers, or pre-emptors as they were called then, had that amount of money. Another difficulty pointed out by Scott was that due to the lack of roads, settlers had to pack on their backs everything they required on their homestead. The produce they wished to sell had to be packed out in a similar fashion. There was a market, now that Prince Rupert was being built on an island near the mainland, but in 1913, the settlers were not producing goods in sufficient quantity to warrant the shipping companies improving their service to the islands.

Ever since gold had been discovered at Mitchell Inlet there had been interest in the potential mineral riches of the islands. Much of the interest remained just that, even though American businessmen bought as much as 20,000 acres of land near Skidegate, thinking this would enable them to tap the islands' fabled coal fields. Nothing came of it. Not until Awaya, Ikeda & Company, a Japanese fishing company based in Vancouver, began to develop property at Ikeda Cove, on Moresby Island, did island mining begin to pay off.

According to the Department of Mines report in 1907, this company employed more than 100 men and a "large and substantially built wharf capable of receiving the largest of the coasting steamships" had been built, as had a tramway connecting the wharf to the mine. By 1908 the company had spent $60,000 developing and upgrading the mine and its equipment. The camp even had telephones, the first on the islands, that connected the mine headquarters to the company offices and the Jedway Hotel at Jedway, a mining centre, a little more than four miles away.

This is the happy side of the Ikeda story. In 1908 "a settlers' association was formed among the people of Lawn Hill and Skidegate, with a membership of forty. Their first meeting resulted in the petitioning of the Provincial Government for a subsidy to run regular steamship schedules to outlying areas. At this meeting a resolution 'to keep this a white man's Island' shows that Asiatic labour was felt to be a problem. In this respect the *Queen Charlotte News* took a stand in favour of white labour, and in the following year conducted something of a crusade to rid the Islands of the Japanese. The Japanese groups were given sixty days in which to quit the Islands. Money spent by them in buying property and erecting houses or business premises at Queen Charlotte City was to be refunded." [2]

In the 1910 edition of the *Annual Report of the Department of Indian Affairs*, the Haida population of Skidegate was listed at 239, that of Masset 372. No wonder these newcomers thought the islands could be made white and kept white. More than anything else, this notion of white supremacy, which was rampant the length and breadth of the coast, led to the Japanese selling their interest in the mine at Ikeda Bay for $250,000. The Vancouver syndicate that bought the mine ran it until 1920, but the war, the transportation difficulties, and the depression that followed the war in British Columbia forced its closure in 1920. It never reopened.

AEROPLANE SPRUCE

As it turned out, for the men and women trying to make a new and better world for themselves in the islands, the enemy was not the hard-working Japanese. The enemy was the world. Soon after war was declared in August 1914, all telegraph communications with the islands was suspended—there was a German cruiser somewhere off the Pacific coast that might benefit from information picked up from wireless operators. The ensuing silence was further deepened when the regular Prince Rupert-Masset steamer ran on the rocks and went out of service for most of August and September.

As soon as world news began to reach the islands late in 1914, men scurried to sign up. One man noted in his diary that he held little hope for the future of the islands. Communications could be shut down momentarily and without warning. All construction and mining had ceased. Nothing would happen on the islands until the war was over; the only thing the settlers—mostly bachelors—could do was enlist and help finish the war, so life could return to normal. Little could he know that the Queen Charlotte Islands' economy was about to boom as never before.

"During the first two years of the war," wrote Roland D. Craig in 1919, "the British Government secured the lumber for aeroplane construction through the Admiralty, or from brokers, as had previously been the custom. Orders for Sitka spruce were all placed in the United States, and, though small amounts of spruce were purchased in British Columbia and Alaska by these United States brokers, the British Government was apparently not aware that British Columbia contained large supplies of the finest aeroplane wood."

Canadian Aeroplanes, Ltd., an aeroplane factory, was built in Toronto by the Imperial Munitions Board in 1917. Because there was little suitable wood available, the manager visited the west coast in search of aeroplane spruce. It had been found, after what were termed "exhaustive tests" in England, that Sitka spruce was "superior to all other woods for the construction of aeroplanes. For this purpose, wood must have a combination of qualities which it is difficult to find. It must be light in weight and...strong. It must have a maximum degree of flexibility, as it is subject to sudden and severe strains, where a rigid or brittle wood is dangerous. It must also be soft in texture, so that it will yield to the impact of bullets without shattering."

Canadian Aeroplanes, Ltd. found the wood and arranged for H.R. MacMillan, formerly British Columbia's chief forester, to buy the necessary spruce. "At the same time the British, French and Italian Governments were experiencing great difficulty in securing sufficient supplies from the United States" and when the U.S. declared war, its "War Department reduced the available supply of spruce for export to an amount which jeopardized the air programmes of the Allies. The Imperial Munitions Board in Canada was then asked to secure, if possible, 24,000,000 feet of aeroplane lumber."

Subsequent research found that there was an estimated 7,781,990,000 board feet of Sitka spruce on Vancouver Island, and another 4,368,695,000 board feet on the coast of the northern mainland. Though this was a tremendous amount of lumber, getting at it was the problem. The Munitions Board had one overwhelming concern in the late fall of 1917—speed. "The necessity for speed in production necessitated concentrating the operations in localities where spruce forms a high percentage of the stand, is easy of access, and where the quality of the timber is high."

Vancouver Island spruce was not only notoriously hard to get, it was poor in quality. Much the same was true for the northern mainland, so far as was known. "On the Queen Charlotte islands, however, spruce is found forming one-third or more of the stand over considerable areas. It is nearly all close to the shore and is undoubtedly of the finest quality to be found on the Pacific coast."

Logging companies moved into the islands and their men were soon busy falling the largest trees in Canada, and getting them into the water. The companies were paid $28 for No. 1 logs, $16 for No. 2. Island mills were improved; two sawmills were built at Masset, and three were set up on Moresby Island. Mills were also built on the mainland at Lakelse and Terrace, Prince Rupert and Skeena City, as the loggers were soon cutting more wood than could be handled by the island sawmills.

By the time the armistice was signed on November 11, 1918, and the majority of the logging contracts were cancelled, 26,124,000 board feet of spruce lumber had been produced, half of this having been cut in the last three months of the war. Impressive as these figures are, logging dealt the first of its many hard blows to the chin

Falling a Sitka spruce, CA 1930s. (COLLECTION OF CHARLES LILLARD)

of the islands' forests. In 1919 it was said that "The supply of Sitka spruce suitable for aeroplane construction is extremely limited....[and the] continuance of cutting on a war basis for another year would have practically exhausted the spruce which could be secured at a reasonable expense of money and effort....Only the large trees contain the clear, fine-grained lumber required, and these cannot be replaced in centuries. Most of the aeroplane material was cut from trees 500 to 800 years old, and it is doubtful if the succeeding stands will ever attain the same quality as these virgin stands." [3]

Port Clements, its name having been changed from Queenstown early in 1914, was a typical coastal logging town by 1918 with a population made up of loggers and mill hands, whores and whisky salesmen. The population of the area is unknown, but at least 800 loggers were said to have worked in the vicinity.

One startling result of all of this activity was a book by D.E. Hatt. Nothing is known of Mr. Hatt's career and life, but in 1918 he was the secretary of the Y.M.C.A. at the Administrative Camp of the Imperial Munitions Board, Department of Aeronautical Supplies, at Thurston Harbour on Talunkwan Island on the east coast of Moresby Island. Hatt's book was *Sitka Spruce* a collection of poetry about the tree, the islands where it grew, and the men who turned the trees into lumber. It was the first book written on the islands, and a book that has not been given its due.

In "Rain" Hatt tells it like it is:

The joys of Charlotte Islands are of the choicest sort,
All through the sunny summer we laugh and hold the fort,
But as the fall advances our bliss is turned to bane,
For only those among us know just how hard it can rain.

And just like every logging poet since, Hatt's men log in spite of hell or high water:

We like to work in comfort as well as any man,
But if we have to rough it you bet your life we can,
And English, Scotch or Irish, Norwegian, Swede or Dane,
We'll keep the logs a-moving in spite of all the rain. [4]

BOOM TO BUST

The war was good to places like Port Clements. In 1919 it was described, in a blurb certainly written months earlier, as a village with a post office, situated 90 miles from Prince Rupert, and serviced by Grand Trunk Pacific steamers such as the *Prince Albert*, the *Prince Charles* and the *Prince John*. The village had a population of 1,000, an Anglican church, a public school, and a Dominion telegraph office. The area was known for its mining, fishing, farming, and logging. Port Clements defined itself as the centre of the production of aeroplane spruce. None of the other island centres had so much to boast of. Skidegate claimed to have 200,000 acres of good soil, though it was mostly covered with trees, and huge banks of dogfish. Tow Hill was described as a mining settlement 20 miles from Masset, possessing such local resources as gold, platinum and tungsten, even though its permanent inhabitants were farmers. There were 30 people living in Tlell and the men were all farmers, but the resources were gold, platinum, and aeroplane spruce. Masset in 1919 was definitely a government centre, and as such there was little to say about the village. Local resources were logging, farming, mining and fishing, which was accurate enough. Even more accurate, and painfully realistic, was the village's population—150.

Two years later the census revealed that "little more than 1,000" people were living on the Queen Charlotte Islands. Apparently these 1,000 were white settlers; if so, to this figure must be added an approximate 600 Haida. This is a 1917 figure and low as it was, 600 was an improvement over the 1915 Department of Indian Affairs census that found only 588 Haida in the islands. Never again would the Haida population be so low. The same cannot be said for the white population.

By 1921 Tow Hill had lost its post office and was being described as a mining settlement. Lawn Hill had a population of 35 in 1928, but the population continued to dwindle until 1930 when it could no longer support a post office. Jedway, which had remained a small but active mining community, lost its post office in 1931. By this time Skidegate was a village of 250 Haida and 50 whites. Nearby Queen Charlotte was a village of 200, mostly loggers and fishermen, plus a few government employees.

A LITERARY REPUTATION

Bad as things looked, for Haida and white alike, the islands proved once again to have more lives than a cat. Another aspect of life among the Haida on the Queen Charlotte Islands was developing. Although there is no evidence suggesting that *Sitka Spruce* had found any more readers than had earlier books about the islands, the popular literary notion of the distant and romantic islands was quietly being reinforced by a series of new books.

First came three books that would prove invaluable to any study of island history. Thomas Crosby's *Up and Down the Pacific Coast* was published in 1914 and, while appealing to a small, coastal audience, found a highly literate and imaginative audience elsewhere. Its readers were those interested in Methodist missionaries, not so much for the religious aspects but as a way of living out adventures vicariously and not having to suffer guilt pangs. W.H. Collison published his *In the Wake of the War Canoe* in 1915 and it went the same directions as had Crosby's, except this time its largest audience was Anglican. Next came Charles Harrison's *Ancient Warriors of the North Pacific* in 1926, published only months before the author's death in London. Harrison's work seemingly sank without a trace, yet the title implies that the author was aiming the book at a known audience.

The Kingdom of the Sun was the next book about the islands. Its author, A.M. Stephen, was a popular British Columbia writer and his books enjoyed national, perhaps even international, circulation. A book that has been reprinted many times and has fascinated generations of young readers was Lurline Bowles Mayol's *The Talking Totem Pole*, which first appeared in the United States in 1930.

The book begins on a high note of romance and mystery and never loses its voice. "The Talking Totem Pole stood in front of the little Samset cabin which nestled close to the tall wind-bent madrona tree and faced the sparkling waters of Puget Sound. Behind the cabin, rose the dark hills covered with dense forest. In front, a little cove stretched crescent-shaped between two rocky headlands, its sandy beach cluttered with masses of driftwood."

Unbeknownst to its readers, this was their first view of a typical Northwest Coast Indian village beach. What follows is equally evocative: "Very, very old was the Totem Pole. Not even the Samsets knew how many years had passed since the strange-looking animals, with huge distorted features, were first carved upon it. They only knew that it had been brought from the northern islands years before by Nawaca's father. He was a famous Haida chief, who had come down to Puget Sound to trade and had remained to live in a country that he found more to his liking than the colder islands of the north." [5]

Sooner or later most boys and girls in the Pacific Northwest saw similar totems on display in Seattle's Pioneer Square, just as children in the midwest visited the Field Museum in Chicago and stood awestruck before the huge totems there. If none of these books were important as literature, they were without question bricks in a facade that delineated the mysteries of the Northwest Coast Indians, of which the Haida on their distant and misty islands were the most mysterious.

Lurline Bowles Mayol published another book in 1933, *The Big Canoe*, and this one was set in the Queen Charlotte Islands. She does not appear to have ever visited the islands, but she had corresponded with one "Chief Edenshaw". She described him, in a private letter dated 1935, as the "grandson of the Chief Edenshaw in these stories [*The Big Canoe*]"; he was, she continues, then living at Masset. "During the fishing season...he will be on the mainland most of the time. He is a very handsome, intelligent man....the photograph which he sent me showed him in dinner clothes, very dignified and immaculate, more like a Japanese statesman than an American Indian." [6]

It is not a dull book, but only part of the book's interest is the text; for many, its real value lies in its illustrations, which were done by W. Langdon Kihn. He would soon become known internationally for his pictorial interpretations of Indian life for the *National Geographic Magazine*. Later, his art would be used to illustrate various Northwest Coast books, as would the work of Walter J. Phillips and Emily Carr.

These artists and many others were all working on the coast in the 1920s and 1930s, but the only person genuinely aware of the importance of their work in those years was Marius Barbeau. And it was during this period that Barbeau did the research that enabled him to write *Haida Carvers in Argillite* and *Haida Myths Illustrated in Argillite Carvings*: books as important to the historian and art critic as they are to the mythologist and ethnologist. The web of the Charlottes was extending in every direction and by the mid-1930s, Emily Carr's paintings of deserted Haida villages were becoming known in the east. Acknowledgement of the importance of Carr's lifelong work had hardly begun when she started writing the books that would make her one of Canada's most popular writers. *Klee Wyck* appeared in 1941 and put places like Cumshewa, Skedans and Tanu on the literary map of Canada. That same year it won the Governor-General's Literary Award for non-fiction, the highest literary accolade Canada has to give.

Inconsequential as much of this writing and art were to island history, they were a major factor in the continued interest in the islands and, arguably, more important to its late 20th-century reputation than were the first 60 years of its 20th-century history. But this growing mythos was only one of the things happening during the 1920s and '30s. It was also a period when the islanders, or those interested in the Queen Charlotte Islands, began to forget about the dream of turning portions of the islands into large farms and ranches. They now turned to logging, mining, and fishing.

DEPRESSION BUSINESS

None of these industries were new to the islands—logging had arrived even before the war—but as with everything else, transportation costs made large-scale logging unprofitable within a few years of the heart going out of the market for spruce. Unprofitable, that is, unless the logging outfit—usually known as "gypos", thus signifying the company was independent of some larger company—also owned its own tug. This is what John R. Morgan did when logging on the east coast of Moresby Island. Another variation of the traditional coastal logging operation was the J.H. Baxter Pole Company that worked in the Mayer Lake-Kumdis Slough area for decades. As small mills were operating at various island locations throughout these years, handloggers or small family logging operations, were able to continue working—if the men supplemented the family income by fishing and hunting. In all likelihood there were dozens of other logging companies working during these years, but the history of island logging has yet to be written. Until such a story is put down on paper, only one thing remains certain: few if any of the larger logging operations added the proverbial thin dime to the economy of places like Masset and Skidegate and Port Clements. This is because the companies hired their crews out of Prince Rupert and Vancouver, bought their supplies in the same places, and sold their timber there. When the companies were forced to shut down in the fall or early winter because of the inclement weather, the loggers, all but a few of whom were single men, wanted to enjoy their summer wages. This was not possible on the Queen Charlotte Islands.

From the 1850s on to the 1940s, mining was a hit-and-miss affair. True, the copper mines at Jedway and Ikeda Cove ran for some time, and apparently successfully enough, but there are no records to verify this. As was usual in the case of dozens of Northwest Coast mining camps, and mining on the islands was no different, only two groups made money in these ventures: prospectors and small developers, who found the deposits and sometimes started mines, and made their profits when they sold the property to mining companies; and the businessmen, who supplied the camps or built the towns, made their money at every turn and knew when to move on to new camps and towns.

There was no serious mining in the islands after the mid-1920s. What did occur was an increased east interest in placer mining, "mostly for claims lying along the sandy north and east shores of Graham Island". This comment undoubtedly refers to the "several local bachelors," reported by a later visitor, who "almost made a scant living panning gold out of the beach". [7] The problem with this work was not in finding the gold, but in keeping it. The gold particles were so fine that it was only with great difficulty that they were separated from the beach sand.

The history of commercial fishing in the islands is a long and complicated story. The first commercial fishing was done by the Haida who supplied dogfish to the Skidegate Oil Company in the 1870s. Halibut fishing commenced locally, with absolutely no effect on the islands, when the *Oscar and Hattie*, a U.S. fishing schooner from the east coast, discovered the halibut banks in Dixon Entrance in 1887. Although islanders began to plead for more stringent enforcement of the three-mile limit as early as 1909, by this time most of the larger halibut schooners, sailing out of Seattle and

*Placer gold mining on the beach, east coast of Graham Island. (*FROM PLACER-MINING IN BRITISH COLUMBIA, *1931)*

134

The halibut steamer NEW ENGLAND, *brought around from the east coast in 1898.*
(COURTESY VANCOUVER MARITIME MUSEUM)

Vancouver, were fishing in the Gulf of Alaska and the Bering Sea. When the Grand Trunk Railway reached Prince Rupert, the town was on its way to becoming "the halibut capital of the world," but this was no reflection on the local fisheries; it was merely that refrigerated railway cars made it possible to ship halibut east from there, saving the schooners the trip to Vancouver and Seattle.

Whaling stations were established at Rose Harbour, Kunghit Island, in 1909 or 1910, and at Naden Harbour, Graham Island, in 1911 or 1912. For a few years whaling was big business in British Columbia, but, like the fur seal and the sea otter, whales were soon almost extinct in the vicinity of the islands. Smaller companies could no longer afford to remain in the business and sold out to larger concerns, so by 1918 coastal whaling was in the hands of one company. In 1928 all the BC stations had been closed except for those in the islands, and these were shut down in 1941.

Economically, the operation and eventual closing of the stations had little effect on the islanders. Both stations were self-sufficient, as were the logging camps of the same period, and sailors, like loggers, rarely spend their money in villages that have nothing more to offer than church meetings and semi-monthly movies.

Between 1909 and the 1950s, salmon salteries and canneries, cold-storage plants, fish-meal works, oil and fertilizer plants, black-cod

A harpoon gun used for whaling, 1908. (COURTESY BCARS)

fishing companies, and clam canneries sprang up at a surprising number of east-coast locations. None of these operations survived. The depression hit the fishing business hard, especially in isolated areas like the Queen Charlotte Islands where transportation costs were already high. The salmon industry was extremely competitive; the salmon packers who opened canneries or related businesses on the islands did not have the financial backing available to the larger companies working at the mouths of the Skeena and Fraser rivers. The islands lacked the salmon runs, the fishing fleet and the manpower resources to attract large-scale investment. By the late 1940s the fishing fleets operating out of island ports sold their catch to buyers, who in turn transported the fish to the mainland where they were processed.

WORLD WAR II AND AFTER
Throughout the 1940s the remaining whites on the islands were only holding their own against escalating transportation costs, shrinking markets and little government assistance. By the time World War II was coming to a predictable conclusion, Queen Charlotte had three stores, a hotel, and one hospital. It was a roaring time: most summer weekends the village was bustling with loggers and fishermen, most of whom could find no way to spend their

wages, and some newcomers thought this was the way it had always been in the islands. During these years there was little contact of any sort between the Haida villages, and not much more between the white villages, most of which were little more than ragtag clusters of shacks. There was not even a high school on the islands.

In 1953 a writer for the provincial government outlined the war years in the islands. "When, in 1936, the international situation became more threatening, the Dominion Government began to seriously consider its Pacific Coast defences. Up to that time the Royal Canadian Air Force had only the one station, that of Vancouver, on the western seaboard. It was then decided to establish an advanced base on the Queen Charlotte Islands. A suitable site was selected on Moresby Island, at Alliford Bay in Skidegate Inlet. An area of about 160 acres was purchased in 1937, and the following year the development of a seaplane base was begun. This work was still in progress when the Second World War broke out.

"The base at Alliford Bay was ready for operations early in 1940, and in May the first aeroplanes were flown north from Vancouver to the new station. Here, with replacements of twin-engined flying-boats in 1941 and long-range Cansos and Catalinas in 1943, routine work continued until the end of the war. This consisted of anti-submarine patrols, transporting personnel and supplies to many spots on the coast, and photographing vital areas. Thus for five years the station was a key point in the Dominion's West Coast defences. It was finally closed in September, 1945." [8]

Ever since the war there have been stories of how, at the head of inlets on the isolated and unexplored west coast, the Imperial Japanese Army set up logging camps that worked for the emperor's cause throughout the war. Another story, long current, tells of how one east-coast cannery was actually a submarine base for the German navy. That no evidence in support of either story was ever found means nothing; thousands of Japanese were moved into what amounted to concentration camps in 1942 for reasons that even at the time, were known to be purely racist.

What really happened was that the war passed the islands by. The invasion of the Aleutian Islands by the Japanese took place too far north to affect island life, the one enemy submarine known to have entered British Columbia waters shelled Estevan Lighthouse on Vancouver Island and then turned homeward, and the Allied invasion of the Aleutians set out from Prince Rupert in 1943, by which time any thought of the war reaching the Northwest Coast had long vanished.

The first post-war visitor to the islands known to have recorded his impressions was Ed Ricketts. In 1946 he found Masset a small community of 50, maybe 100, houses and a few hundred people a bit south of Old Masset. Masset had a post office, two stores, and several power plants that supplied electricity to the community. There were no medical facilities and no water or sewage system, but there was a school, a hotel and a community hall. "The government is represented by a provincial police with a small station, by the postmaster, who is also the customs man, by the Indian agent and by a road superintendent." Ricketts was unsure of the roads, though he did note the famous plank road that ran out from Masset to Tow Hill. There at low tide, he was told, cars could be driven safely at any speed on the hard-packed sand. At the time of Ricketts' brief visit there were only two cars in Masset, both owned by the local taxi driver; as well there were "several" trucks.

"At Old Massett, there's a cannery owned by Nelson Brothers which is leased out to the co-op. The co-op shares the cannery with a private enterprise outfit, and what the working arrangement is I can't imagine. The private outfit packs crab and they have a very fine collecting boat, about a 50' job, I'd say, diesel. The co-op is Indian-white, it cans razor clams, and on the low tides most of the town turns out, men, women and children, Indians and whites (altho there's something of a color line here, not much), and get into trucks to the clamming grounds, everyone gets busy with shovel at piece-work rates. The only other local production is from the fisheries."

By "fisheries" Ricketts meant salmon fishing. However, since the fishermen sold to buying boats from Prince Rupert, and as most of the fishermen appeared to be from the mainland, there was "little local contact" so far as he could tell.

Mail reached Masset every two weeks. Even though there were sporadic airline connections to Vancouver, the airline had no mail contract. Something else that Ricketts noted, which appears to have been a long-term situation, was that island centres had little contact with one another, except through Prince Rupert. This isolation had begun early in the century when the northern and southern Haida chose to go their own ways. By the time of World War II, there was virtually no contact between the Haida of Skidegate and those of Masset. The first European settlers did not ignore each other; associations were formed that brought them together, and it was the dream of each village and settlement that roads would be built to make it possible for everyone to move about freely. This did not happen.

Roads were not built, settlers without capital found clearing and draining land to be a next-to-impossible task, and then came the depression and the war. The remaining whites found it less time consuming and more profitable to make the 80-mile trip to Prince Rupert than to visit one another. The mother of one woman Ricketts saw at Masset had not left the family homestead for several years and had not been off the islands in 30 years.

The people Ricketts encountered called themselves fishermen and farmers, but there was little farming going on and nearly all the food consumed by the islanders at that time was being imported from Prince Rupert. There were cows, but he was told that it was difficult to keep them alive through the winter. As only the two stores in Masset had refrigeration, fresh meat and vegetables were a treat. Rickett relates how people rushed to the stores on boat day to buy all the meat and perishables they could, which was a limited amount due to war-time food rationing still being in effect. On boat-day night everyone would have huge meals, then smaller meals for the next day or so until the food was gone or had gone bad and had to be thrown out, at which time they would return to eating venison, fish and clams. "If they'd get together on some system of cooperation and leave the stuff under refrigeration until they're ready for it, they'd have half again as much meat."

The water situation was something else that intrigued Ricketts. "But here again in this rain-drenched country, running water's the chief problem. We were fortunate in renting a place that had a sink and flush toilet. We very naively used up all the water in a few hours and had to wait for rain replacements. Very clever householder had rigged up two 50-gallon barrels fed by rain from the roof....we got to flushing the toilet with sea water, and from the number of buckets this fellow had around, I assume he depended on the ocean...for most purposes that didn't require fresh water." [9]

ROADS

Island transportation was often difficult and sometimes unique right up until the late 1950s. The first island road connecting two settlements any distance apart was the private plank road from Masset to Tow Hill, which was built by laying planks over stringers or deadmen so as to form two narrow platforms for an automobile's wheels. How many cars were available to use this road is unknown, but as late as 1946 it was being used by locals with bicycles outfitted with special sidecars. This plank-road concept worked so well that the provincial government built a similar road between Port Clements and Tlell. In short order this road became a favourite subject for visiting photographers. Work on construction of a proper road to replace this wooden track began in 1941, but was not completed for another decade. Not until 1958 was there a road between Port Clements and Masset.

THE GOLDEN YEARS

The economic boom that began in the early 1950s caught many British Columbians by surprise. A depression had followed World War I and the government was prepared for the worst, but the worst that happened was that politicians who had held office for decades were voted out. What happened in most areas of the province during the 1950s and '60s is well-documented; not so in the islands. It is as though the islands had slipped from view, probably because the only boom on the islands was directly related to the complete exploitation of the Queen Charlotte Islands' forests. As late as 1956 the islands had only 3,082 inhabitants, 1,500 of whom were Haida, and few amenities. There were schools, a hospital at Queen Charlotte, and government offices at Masset. The fishing fleet was minute. Prospecting was being done but there was little mining. There were 2,100 acres of farm land, but less than a quarter of this acreage was cultivated. The island was completely reliant on imported goods.

In 1958, when BC celebrated its centenary, the islands were ignored. One official directory of the celebrations left the islands off its map. A pageant-style popular history of the province published at this time, to commemorate the hundred-year anniversary, mentions Perez's sighting of the islands and turns its attention elsewhere. The silence even extends to the first history of the islands published in 1968. All but one of the major travel books written about British Columbia in the late 1940s and throughout the 1950s ignored the islands, probably because they were difficult to reach and once there, travel writers realized there was little to write about. If a writer wanted to see "totem pole Indians," it was easier to see them at Prince Rupert or on Vancouver Island; logging could be studied close up at dozens of Vancouver Island locations; the Fraser and Skeena rivers offered salmon and fishing fleets and canneries.

Historical writers were little better—and with far fewer excuses. The bible of British Columbia history, Margaret Ormsby's *British Columbia: A History*, which has been a textbook to three generations of B.C. students, only rarely mentions the islands and then only as geographical points. The Haida get shorter shrift: they are never mentioned. Subsequent histories are little better, though some do admit the Haida exist.

But the story had begun to change elsewhere, and would soon change on the islands. Emily Carr's fame was growing and her books were read wherever English was spoken. There was a growing interest in Northwest Coast history and art. In 1947 Marius Barbeau had begun to survey, photograph and salvage as many of the Haida poles as still stood in the long-deserted villages. This work drew the attention of Harry B. Hawthorn, of the University of British Columbia's Department of Anthropology and Sociology, and Hawthorn's wife, Audrey Hawthorn, curator of UBC's Museum of Anthropology, such as it was in those days.

Not long after this, one of the legendary figures associated with the story of Northwest Coast culture entered the story. This was Wilson Duff, then curator of anthropology at British Columbia's Provincial Museum. Duff led a "major salvage operation" to the village of Ninstints in 1957 and was accompanied by Harry Hawthorn, Michael Kew, Wayne Suttles, John Smyly and Bill Reid. The immediate result was the rescue of portions or entire lengths of 23 totems. In the short term this drew attention to the plight of Ninstints, long abandoned, overgrown, windswept and rain soaked, and open to

Old totems at Ninstints, 1970s. (COURTESY JAMES TUOHY)

vandalism, and led to the site being declared a provincial park in 1958. In 1981, it was made a World Heritage Site by UNESCO.

Marius Barbeau went on to write two important books about Haida art and three on totems, one of which—the two-volume *Totem Poles*—contained everything then known about Haida totems. Wilson Duff would write papers on Haida art and was a constant theorizer, who encouraged an entire generation of Northwest Coast carvers. Michael Kew would become the director of the University of British Columbia's Museum of Anthropology and lead it on to international fame. John Smyly, with his wife Carolyn, would write *Those Born at Koona*, a book that recreates the village of Koona, better known as Skedans. And Bill Reid, a CBC announcer in 1957, would become the world's best-known Haida artist.

In 1957 these men knew that they were doing something vitally important by rescuing the poles of Ninstints, but they could not know that they were ushering in an entirely new era for the Haida and Haida Gwaii—their beloved islands.

Old totem at Skedans, 1978. (COLLECTION OF CHARLES LILLARD)

CHAPTER EIGHT

HAIDA GWAII

A NEW DAY

THE STORY of the Queen Charlotte Islands reached another of its turning points in 1969. In August of that year, the first totem pole to be carved at Haida (Masset) within living memory was raised, and a pole-raising potlatch, to which 600 guests were invited was held to celebrate and honour the occasion. The carver, 22-year-old Robert Davidson, was the great-grandson of Charles Edenshaw, who is still considered the greatest of traditional Haida carvers, and the grandson of Florence Edenshaw Davidson, one of the truly wise Haida elders. Called the Bear Mother Pole, it consisted of three grizzly bears, a frog and small human figures, with the traditional three watchmen sitting atop the pole. It was reminiscent of Edenshaw's Grizzly Bear Pole that once stood at Klaskun Point near Tow Hill and belonged to Chief Albert Edward Edenshaw.

Chief Weah (William Matthews) greeted the visitors to the ceremony, which was held within a few yards of the Anglican church. Had they been invited, the spirits of Reverends Collison and Harrison would have rejoiced: they had loved the Haida and this was a sure sign their work had not been in vain.

For Masset the raising of the Bear Mother Pole was an event of unparalleled significance, and yet the totem was another sign that Haida individualism had lost none of its power. The pole was the dream of Robert Davidson; it was not a village dream, nor was it a village project. Masset did not finance the work either; that was done

143

to a large extent by a grant from the Canadian government. A final irony was that the carver had learned most of his skills in Vancouver and had not lived in the islands for some years.

Only seven years earlier, in 1962, a national weekly magazine had run a series of articles on the Indians of Canada. The second article in this series was entitled "The Haidas, Empire Builders Turned Slum Dwellers," and a cutline opined: "They were once a mighty people—owners of slaves, creators of magnificent totem art. Today they are a defeated and displaced people." Since there were no longer photographically impressive totems standing at Skidegate, the lead photograph accompanying this article showed Kwakiutl totems at Alert Bay. "The Haidas," the author of this article went on to say, "on the island that was once the headquarters of their Pacific empire, are subject in their daily lives not only to the awful monotony of poverty but to an accumulation of indignities—afflictions from which refugees characteristically suffer."

Badly off as they were, the Haida were not without courage. Only a few months earlier a truck carrying 30 people from Masset to their jobs in a nearby cannery went off the road, injuring several and killing a young woman. The driver of the truck, a white employed by the cannery, was charged with driving without due care and attention and was fined $200. The cannery, owner of the truck, which did not have licence plates, was fined $25. "When the cannery insisted on keeping the offending driver...[the] Haida cannery workers and fishermen went on strike. With the strength of United Fishermen and Allied Workers' unions behind them, they won." The cannery fired the driver.

"In less than a decade its [Masset's] population has almost doubled. But during the same period fishing, the Haidas' only occupation, has declined. With only seasonal work available in an industry which steadily employs more machines and few human hands, the Haidas are incapable of improving their own lot. They subsist on federal welfare allowances and pensions and they suffer from a feeling of being steadily squeezed back by a white majority that rules their lives and is utterly indifferent to their fate." [1]

ANOTHER WRITER REPORTS

The year Davidson's pole was raised, Kathleen E. Dalzell published her *Queen Charlotte Islands, 1774-1966*, a history as well as a celebration of the islands' European and Asian pioneers. Dalzell, the daughter of early-day pioneers, told their story in *The Beloved Island*, a biographical memoir 20 years later. The final chapter of her history provides a statistical outline of the islands in 1966.

Her first point attempts to put the human population into perspective. John Work finished compiling his census of the islands in 1841, at which time there were 12 major villages and 6,693 Haida. In 1966 there were again 12 settlements, and a possible population of 5,000 people. The settlements were Old Masset, New Masset, Juskatla Camp, Tlell, Skidegate Mission, Port Clements, Skidegate Landing, Queen Charlotte City, Sandspit, Moresby Camp, Tasu, and Jedway. The largest of these villages was Old Masset with 1,000 people; Sandspit and Queen Charlotte City had 500 residents each, and Tasu, a west-coast mining-company town under construction, was expected to have 1,000 residents soon.

Although Dalzell's breakdown of locations and populations are accurate enough, the picture is somewhat more complex than her sketch admits. In 1966, Old Masset was a large but scattered settlement without a steamer landing or post office. Officially, Masset was the village and the only such incorporated place on the islands. Skidegate Landing was correctly known as Skidegate, and it consisted of a post office and steamer landing; Skidegate Mission was the surrounding settlement. Moresby Camp was a steamer landing and Juskatla a settlement. Sandspit and Queen Charlotte ("city" was not then officially part of the name) were both described by the government as small and compact settlements with a post office and steamer landing, as was Port Clements. Tlell was similar to these three places with the exception that it lacked a steamer landing. Tasu was not officially recognized, as it was a construction/mining camp at the time. Jedway was a location with a steamer landing and a post office that, after a 31-year closure, had been reopened in 1962, and would be closed again in 1968.

In 1967 the provincial government described the Queen Charlotte Islands Area as comprised "by School District No. 50 with an area of 3,887 square miles and a population of 2,121 persons (1961). It includes the Village of Massett (1961 population 547) and the communities of Moresby (139), Sandspit (466) and Juskatla (214)." [2] The estimated population four years later was 2,900, down a little more than 100 persons from the 1956 census. The discrepancy between these figures and Dalzell's (even when the projected Tasu population is subtracted) is due to seasonal labour—Dalzell's head-counting was done in October, before the logging camps, and the many mining and construction sites, closed for the season.

Logging was still the islands' major industry in 1966, employing some 650 people. Fishing came next. A fleet of 180 fishing boats called Masset home, and 290 people either fished or worked in the local cannery.

HOLES IN THE GROUND

In 1966, mining was finally going somewhere, or would as soon as the $25,000,000 development at the Tasu copper-iron mine went into production. At that time there were plans afoot for a company to develop the sphagnum peat moss deposits near Masset and Port Clements. This bright picture did not last. By 1986 only five people were involved in mining. Jedway, run by Jedway Iron Ore Ltd. had closed in 1968. Tasu, a townsite and mill owned and operated by Wesfrob Mines Ltd., had begun shipping concentrates in August 1967. Originally an open-pit operation, it had begun underground operations in 1973, but nothing could save it from the fact that the mine was running out of ore. Late in 1983 Wesfrob closed down its operation at Tasu.

Commercial fishing had not developed to any extent throughout the 1970s. Although there were three fish-processing plants on the islands in 1987, and 123 commercial boats, only 210 persons were working in the industry. But these figures are suspect. Elsewhere it is stated that only one of these plants ran in 1987 and at the same time fewer than 175 people were actually involved in the industry as fishermen.

Economically, agriculture and tourism were negligible.

CANOES TO FERRIES

Tourists began moving north from San Francisco as early as the 1870s, the attraction being the already legendary "Seward's Ice Box" that the United States had only recently bought from Russia. Once in Alaska most travellers were hypnotized by the colours and the mountains and the seemingly endless waterways of the Inside Passage. People came back for more; thus certain stops along the BC coast, such as Victoria and Port Simpson, became early-day tourist attractions. In 1892, Haida hunting canoes were available at Port Simpson for between $30 and $50, while travelling canoes could be purchased for $75 to $150. Totems and carvings, baskets and relics, were also available. Masset was then serviced irregularly by Canadian Pacific Navigation steamers, but tourists were advised that the spirit of progress was fast eliminating the village's picturesqueness.

146

Various steamship lines continued to service the Charlottes, but islanders apparently did not consider tourism worth encouraging. In the 1920s, when mainland and Vancouver Island towns and villages were celebrating their "picturesqueness", the Europeans in the islands were looking for investors. This trend continued into the 1960s.

One problem facing potential island tourists was transportation. Getting to the islands by ship could be difficult and time-consuming, as Ed Ricketts had discovered in 1946. At the time of his visit, planes were flying between Vancouver and Masset, but there was no passenger service—unless an islander knew a pilot. Planes could be chartered, but this was an expensive way of travelling. Had Ricketts arrived in the islands a few weeks later, he would have found regular air service available. Jim Spilsbury and his partners, who made frequent flights to the islands to service short-wave radios, started Queen Charlotte Airlines in June 1946. Nine years later it was bought out by Pacific Western Airlines; it still services the islands, but now it is part of Canadian Airlines International, the second-largest airline in Canada.

Air service had made the islands accessible; still, tourism was not encouraged. There were only three hotels in the Queen Charlottes in 1967, and only one of them advertised anything but rooms. But all of this was changing: by 1972 PWA had been joined by Trans-Provincial Airlines. That year Sandspit had one hotel, and its local celebrations were a coho fishing derby and its Labour Day Earwig Races. There was also fishing and deer hunting. Masset, Tlell, Port Clements and Queen Charlotte City each offered fishing and had a hotel apiece. By 1980 some of the hotels had become motels, one motel was now called a "motel-farm", and all their rates had more than doubled. Fishing, Haida art and logging sports were then the major attractions, except at Sandspit where there was a golf course.

All this changed in 1989 when the government initiated ferry service to Skidegate Landing, and Graham Island became the western terminus of Highway 16. Suddenly the islands boasted 12 motels and hotels, guest houses and RV sites. All this led to the provincial government reporting that, even though transportation to the islands was expensive, the tourist "industry is growing as more people become aware of the Islands' many attributes, and the recent establishment of South Moresby National Park Reserve will undoubtedly focus more attention on the area....Attractions include rugged scenery, miles of sandy beach, historic native settlements, and unexcelled hunting and fishing. Game animals include deer, elk and Black

The rugged east coast of Louise Island, with sea lions. (COLLECTION OF CHARLES LILLARD)

bear; the deer are very plentiful and there is no closed season for either sex. Fishing is excellent in both salt water and the rivers. Copper, Deena, Yakoun and Tlell Rivers contain Steelhead, Rainbow and Cut-throat trout and Dolly Varden." [3]

THE VIEW FROM 1990

Tourism should have changed things a great deal, but a government report written in the early 1990s spoke guardedly of the economic situation of the islands. There were two villages in the islands, Masset with a population of 1,529, and Port Clements with 539. Juskatla was a community of 47, Queen Charlotte City (though still a community, "city" was now officially part of its name) of 924, Sandspit had 537 residents and Tlell 152. Officially the population in 1986 was 5,480, a figure down 2.5% from 1981.

"Growth in the early 1970s was largely attributable to the establishment of a Canadian Forces Base at Masset. Since 1976 the population has been relatively stable. Apart from direct and indirect military employment, the economy of the Islands is based almost entirely on resource extraction. Timber harvested in the Area is almost all shipped south for conversion. Mineral exploration, commercial fishing and modest agricultural activity round off the economy. Tourism is believed to have excellent potential but development has been hindered by access problems. In addition, internal transportation problems have hindered development of centralized trade and services.

"Several major resource and service communities exist independently of one another and tend to rely on Mainland sources of supply. Mining has played an important role in the islands' economy in the past and could again if a planned gold mine on Graham Island proceeds as planned. In the longer term, there may be impacts from the service requirements of offshore drilling activity, should that proceed. Logging activity has been constrained by the establishment of South Moresby National Park Reserve in 1987. The park's potential impact on the mines and petroleum sectors has yet to be fully assessed but the former mining town of Tasu will become South Moresby's first tourist resort and a Haida community. As the local Haida are expected to assume the leading role in services related to the park, a population influx is not anticipated in response to tourism development. Nevertheless, the federal government is committed to an expenditure of $106 million over eight years to build tourism facilities, improve transportation and related services, support small business development, and enhance forest management." [4]

In 1986 there were 620 people involved in logging on the islands, and the companies involved in the industry were MacMillan Bloedel Ltd., Fletcher Challenge Canada Ltd., and Western Forest Products Ltd. These companies all operated large permanent camps: MacMillan Bloedel at Juskatla, Fletcher Challenge at Sandspit, and Western Forest Products at Moresby Camp. Due to the legislation passed to save the southern portion of Moresby Island from logging, there was little chance that logging could look forward to future growth. There were no sawmills operating on the islands at that time, despite the BC Forest Service advertising "special sales conditional upon the establishment of local milling facilities." [5] Good as this might have sounded on paper, everyone in the sawmill business knew of the islands' isolation, and the costs and difficulties involved in transporting the finished products to island and mainland markets.

Distance, climate, drainage, and the cost of clearing land were all, as they had been from as early as 1909, cited as reasons why agriculture on Graham Island's lowlands could only be regarded as unsuccessful. The government reported that the total "farm capital value was estimated at $3.7 million and sale receipts for 1985 at $95,447." However, of the islands' 12 farms, only three "reported sales of more than $10,000." [6]

ART SURVIVES

Dreary and downtrodden as Masset appeared to one journalist in 1962, there was one ray of light. "In three Haida households, all inter-related, the old talent for carving in wood and argillite—a slate material quarried near Skidegate—is a source of supplementary income. Robert Davidson, at 86, earns $10.50 an inch for his argillite totems, most of which stand 12 inches high. A 15-year-old grandson, another Robert, is already a skilled carver." Victor Adams, a son-in-law, was also a carver, but good as these men were, the prices for their work were low—$500 for a storage chest representing an entire winter's work. Like everyone else in the family Adams fished during the summer. "The Davidson-Adams clan has done well out of fishing and invested the proceeds in middle-class respectability. Robert Davidson's 13-room house is the grandest in the whole area." [7]

One aspect of the survival of Haida carving has been largely forgotten. An Anglican minister at Skidegate, one Reverend L. Hooper, attempted to revive 'stonecarving'. He found two carvers in 1951 and by 1954 there were eight carvers at Skidegate. "Books with illustrations of ancient myths were made available, and when it became possible to obtain advances still more men became inter-ested." It was the minister's idea to form a union, which he felt would make the argillite carvings more saleable. If this union gained enough strength, it could also deal with the sale of imitations—such as the carvings made by one Tsimshian whose Haida contacts were selling him argillite. Hooper also tried to set up discussion groups where the myths and motifs and other mutual interests of the carvers could be discussed.

Little came of this effort. Hooper was transferred and most of the Haida could make better wages in the logging camps than at a carver's table. Rufus Moody was one of the few Haida who stuck to carving and in 1965 "he gave demonstrations of his skill in a large department store in Vancouver, and in 1966 he carved the second largest argillite totem pole ever made by a Haida; this pole had a height of 50 inches and was intended for the House of Commons at Ottawa." [8]

During these same years Bill Reid, already considered the foremost Haida artist of his generation, was involved in the construction of the totem village at the University of British Columbia, while other Haida carvers created a pole for Expo—the World Expedition—at Montreal in 1967. It only seems natural now that the next, and logical, step two years later in this rebirth of Haida carving would be the raising of the Bear Mother Pole.

HIPPIES

About the time that Robert Davidson began carving his totem in 1968, the youthful counterculture movement, which had been sweeping east and north across North America from San Francisco for 16 months, reached the Queen Charlotte Islands. On the Northwest Coast the hippie-flower children movement had its parallels with the pioneering movement, which had tried to civilize the west and north coasts of Vancouver Island and the Queen Charlottes before and after World War I. The majority of the men and women in both groups were young, white, and middle-class. Few of these people had rural experience. Both groups found out that the frontier is a hostile place and only those who truly wish to turn their backs on civilization can live off the country.

However, both pioneers and hippies were part of a culture that believes in frontiers, and neither one wanted to believe that there are places so close to cities like Prince Rupert and Ketchikan that cannot be inhabited. To inhabit a place is to be part of that place, but neither the pioneers or the hippies really inhabited the islands: they merely lived there, ultimately becoming part of the labour pool or support force.

Those who stayed, just like their counterparts on Vancouver Island and the Gulf Islands farther south, rapidly became an extension of the local communities. But few of these people blended in with the old

Floathouses at Queen Charlotte City, 1970s. (COLLECTION OF CHARLES LILLARD)

timers; they had known prosperity, Europe and Asia, and many of them came from well-to-do homes and possessed educations the likes of which had previously been unknown on the islands. People with such backgrounds found living on the islands quite impossible. They had been willing to return to the land and work; they were unwilling to live without the culture they felt was both their inheritance and their right.

By 1980, it became obvious to all who cared to look at the 20th-century history of the islands that the Queen Charlotte Islands were in the unique position of lying west of the frontier. They were, very much like a great deal of Alaska, and almost all of the northern portion of British Columbia, uninhabitable at that time. Satellites was what they were, satellites revolving around and totally dependent on mainland politics and economics. Greenland was a case in point. The European Greenlanders did quite well as long as they could depend on Iceland and Denmark, but when their lifelines broke down, so did the two Greenland colonies. Today's islanders living in communities on the islands of Southeastern Alaska, and the much less remote islands of the Strait of Georgia and Puget Sound, are totally dependent on government-funded transportation, such as ferries and airlines. Every one of these places is a bedroom community, a suburb or a retirement centre for the few large nearby towns and cities.

ARTISTS AND WRITERS

One of the first post-war books about the Queen Charlotte Islands to reach a large audience was *Roar of the Breakers*. Written by Alan Morley, a Vancouver-based journalist, it was the biography of the Reverend Peter Reginald Kelly, D.D., a long-time Methodist minister who later became head of the United Church in British Columbia. The Reverend Kelly was the scion of an aristocratic Haida family from Skidegate.

Whether the author knew it or not, this was the fourth book about life in the islands, and, like all other such books, Morley's was written on the mainland. Leaving the islands to write was becoming a Queen Charlottes' tradition, which is understandable, for at the time there were few island writers.

The islands always attracted the young. Most of the young in the years since World War II were boys and young men, who went north to work in logging camps. Others went north to fish and some to work in mining or surveying camps. The money was good in the 1950s and '60s, and as there was absolutely nowhere to spend summer wages the islands were a good place to make a grubstake. In the 1960s the islands began to attract another sort of young person: artists and writers, and none of these people were part of the counter-culture movement.

Benita Sanders and Helen Piddington went to the islands to paint in the 1960s. Writers such as Susan Musgrave, Sean Virgo, Brian Brett, and J. Michael Yates followed in the 1970s; all lived and wrote in the islands for several years. But leaving the islands to write about the islands continued as a tradition. Some years after leaving the Queen Charlottes, Yates wrote *Insel*, a collection of meditations about the islands; most of the poems in Virgo's *Deathwatch at Skidegate Narrows* are about his time there, but appear to have been written elsewhere; likewise Musgrave's *The Charcoal Burners*, something of a gothic novel about life on the islands. In one of the most incongruous moves in Canadian literature, Yates would attempt to operate Sono Nis Press, which specialized in avant-garde and ultra-contemporary poetry, from Port Clements.

During these years at least one person of the older generation was trying to give her beloved islands a literary shape. In 1973 the second of what would eventually become a trilogy of histories about the islands was published by Kathleen Dalzell. Her books probably did as much to popularize the islands as did any other single thing. She put island history, which had not been collected up to that point, between covers and made it readable. Another book to appear at this time was Neil G. Carey's *A Guide to the Queen Charlotte Islands*. This was followed by numerous other books about the islands, past and present. Taken together, these books did have an effect on the islands.

There was something unique about the Queen Charlotte Islands. For Dalzell it was the pioneer history. Virgo and Yates were alternately baffled and horrified by the natural world, one that had turned out to be something quite different from the Wordsworthian isolation and splendour they had seemingly expected.

Carey was fascinated by the tourist potential. And for Bill Reid, whose *Out of the Silence*, a meditation over photos of North Coast totems in situ was published in 1971, the people of the coast and the Queen Charlotte Islands "centered their society around what was to them the essence of life: what we now call 'art'." [9]

Perhaps the only writer during this period to get the islands into focus, and probably the only writer to have done so since the days of Emily Carr, was W.O. Turner, an American writer of westerns. For all of the pulp-fiction elements in *Call the Beast thy Brother*, Turner did catch the essence of what had existed on the Queen Charlotte Islands. Turner portrayed a culture created by a humorous and intelligent people, who lived a rough and day-by-day existence on the outside fringe of Northwest Coast. Although it is not a particularly good novel, it is a clear-eyed look into the landscape of the Queen Charlotte Islands at about the time smallpox would close the doors to the future for unknown thousands of Haida.

FARMLAND TO PARKLAND

The next event of consequence had a direct link to the pole at Masset, the hippies and the artists and writers. It was another aspect of the changing times and the growing respect for nature on the Northwest Coast. In 1973 the provincial government established Naikoon Provincial Park, which took up most of the northeast portion of Graham Island.

The government would later write: "Like all parts of Haida Gwaii—the Queen Charlotte Islands—the park area has a long history of occupation and use by the Haida people and figures prominently in their present lifestyle and legends. It is part of the Haida Nation's comprehensive land claim." The area also has a 150-year white history, starting with the HBC ships that went aground on Rose Spit, and ending with the settlers who spent most of their century living in the area that is now park.

People have been known to spend days just drifting through the aspects of the island world to be found in Naikoon Park. The rainforest, with the silence and the heavy clinging green that everywhere reminds one that this is another world, and one that man does not move through comfortably, is the closest thing to jungle that can be found in the Pacific Northwest. This area is the only park to contain examples of the Queen Charlotte Lowlands; it also has "some of the most extensive sand dunes in Canada" and "the best examples of Sitka spruce dune forests in BC". It is a wonderland. Three-quarters of the 230 species of birds reputed to have been seen on the islands were sighted inside the park. It is also the home of the sea mertensia, a bluebell found on the sand dunes, which exists nowhere else in British Columbia.

Like so many other places representing the Haida-European past of the Queen Charlotte Islands, Naikoon Park is a bundle of contradictions. Numerous rare plants and animals exist alongside such imports as feral dogs, rabbits, raccoon, cows and beaver. Although its

Haida history is ancient, and its European history is a century old, neither Haida nor white did much inside the park within historical times. The village of Hiellen was situated on the east bank of the Hiellen River within the shadow cast by Tow Hill, "a columnar basaltic rock scoured by glacial ice into a classic roche moutonnee".

Early in the 1860s the village was burned to the ground by Tsimshian raiders and never rebuilt, its residents settling in Masset. The people of Masset now own the small Indian Reserve where Hiellen stood. Tow Hill was a something of a settlement from about 1913 to 1921. Later it was known as a mining community, but the only mining of any importance done in the area was placer mining on the beaches. None of this was ever successful, nor were the attempts to drill for oil. At one point Tow Hill was the location of a clam cannery, which operated only long enough to become a failure. Logging and sawmilling operations were carried out within the boundaries of what is now the park, but the only logging of lasting importance was the pole logging done around Mayer Lake at various times between the 1920s and 1960s. The end of the story was told in a draft of a report about the background of the park in 1992.

"A few families remained within the park working their land. These included members of the Carpenter family living a few miles west of Rose Spit until 1939 and Harry Crooks at White Creek until 1971. Bob Beitush farmed at the mouth of the Tlell River from 1912 until his death in 1964. A number of pre-emptions became crown land grants and are private holdings within the park today. There are visible reminders of these settlements and old fence posts, sections of corduroy roads, clearings, drainage ditches, and collapsed houses can still be found. The settlers named many of the places within the park and one outstanding natural feature, the Oceanda River, was permanently altered when it changed course and now flows in the drainage ditch dug in 1925." [10] This ditch was a cooperative effort of a group of settlers and by the time the work was done it was 600 feet long and ten feet wide. It did not change history: the settlers failed to break the land; the pink, coho and chum salmon, which spawned in the river before it moved into the ditch, spawn there yet.

SOUTH MORESBY

Another event arising from the growing awareness of the Haidas and the whites on the Queen Charlotte Islands was the creation of the South Moresby/Gwaii Haanas National Park Reserve. A wall poster dating from 1977 states the early position of those who dedicated a tremendous amount of time and energy to what was then termed the Southern Moresby Wilderness Proposal.

"In the southern part of the Queen Charlotte Archipelago...there exists a unique and unspoiled microcosm of the Canadian Pacific Coast. Few areas in the world provide the opportunity to preserve so much wilderness coastline with such variety of landforms and wealth of living creatures. The proposed 550 square mile Southern Moresby Wilderness is smaller in area than 8 existing B.C. provincial parks, yet contains over 650 miles of coastal shoreline—more coastline than is now protected in all B.C. parks and reserves combined. The area features the highest energy coastline in Canada, an island with a near-boiling mineral spring, shellfish beds of phenomenal productivity, and the largest rookeries of sea lions on the Canadian Pacific Coast. Forests containing some of the world's largest remaining Red Cedar, Yellow Cypress [yellow cedar], and Sitka Spruce trees form a green tapestry across an area with 95% virgin cover.

"In 1974, Rayonier of Canada Ltd., a subsidiary of I.T. & T., applied for a permit to begin massive clearcut logging in the very heart of this region. The Skidegate Band Council of the Haida Indians opposed these plans for fear that traditional food resources and ancestral village sites would be damaged or destroyed. At the same time, the Islands Protection Committee was formed to act as an environmentally concerned voice for all Queen Charlotte Islands residents. The Southern Moresby Wilderness Proposal in its first draft was submitted to the Provincial Government in October 1974, and over 20% of the adult population of the Queen Charlottes signed their names to a petition calling for an immediate moratorium on logging in the Area until detailed environmental studies were conducted." [11]

As of 1977 the government had done nothing and logging continued "within the region at an alarming rate." By 1985 people were saying, "If we don't conserve South Moresby, our children will have to go to Alaska to catch a glimpse of what Coastal BC once looked like." Haida protests on Lyell Island focussed world attention on the land that they and many others were trying to save from chain saws and pulp mills. During the winter of 1985-86 the provincial government created the Wilderness Advisory Committee, and although this committee made several recommendations, nothing happened.

At this point the federal government began to react in the face of the national and international attention the work of the Haida and the environmentalists was attracting. Two years later, in July 1987, the Memorandum of Understanding was signed, which led directly to the 1988 signing of the South Moresby Agreement. This made it possible for the federal government to designate South Moresby a national park reserve.

By 1990 the land had been set aside as a park reserve and the logging companies were gone. Details had yet to be settled, i.e. the area's name: would it be Gwaii Haanas, which is what the Haida called it, or South Moresby, the English—and very British—name? The way the area was to be used was also open to question. As there were more than 100 mining claims in the park, it was possible, though unlikely, that mines would be developed inside the park reserve's boundaries; offshore oil drilling was another possibility. Even the manner in which tourists would be able to use the area was undecided as of 1990. No roads were planned, and "improvements", whatever that may mean, were going to be strictly monitored.

Since the park reserve was created, thousands of boaters and tourists have visited Gwaii Haanas/South Moresby. How long this will last is open to question. Even as early as 1988 there was trouble with pollution, helicopter traffic, and the over-use of some areas. What is left of the ruined villages such as Ninstints is very fragile, and how people will be able to visit the ruins, and not destroy them and the surrounding vegetation in the process, is a question no one has answered.

ANCIENT RESIDENTS RETURN

In the 100 years or so that the Northwest Coast people over-hunted the sea otter to satisfy American, British and Russian fur traders, it is believed that as many as 10,000 to 15,000 of the animals were killed yearly. Estimates vary, but it seems that between 800,000 and 1,000,000 sea otter were killed in Alaska during the years it was owned by Russia. Otter skins were big business ($50,000,000 to the Russians in the 18th century) and even after the fur traders moved on, the sea otters were hunted; the prices paid in China for their pelts were astronomical—$2,000 for one pelt in 1900.

In 1911 the Queen Charlotte Islands were home to one of the 13 sea otter colonies still known to exist; the others were in Alaska and California, Russia and Mexico. It was in this same year that Britain, Japan, the United States and Russia signed the Fur Seal Treaty, which also protected the sea otter. Two years later the U.S. created a national wildlife refuge area in the Aleutian Islands where there were known to be sea otter colonies. None of this protected the sea otter completely. Certain Russian islands had not been part of the agreement and controlled hunting was allowed there until 1924.

Either four or six years earlier poachers had killed the last sea otter in the Queen Charlotte Islands somewhere near North Island. That was that. Although poachers continued to kill sea otter in Alaska, World War II changed things: humans began killing each other. In the Aleutians, where guards had been protecting the animals since 1936, one of the two sea otter colonies in North America began to expand. As early as 1958 there were sightings of sea otter in the vicinity of Cape St. James, but much of the British Columbia coast remained empty. In 1969, and again in 1970 and 1972, Alaskan sea otter were set free on the west coast of Vancouver Island. This increased the number of sightings, but even as late as 1984 there were so few on the northern coast of the province that another transfer of Alaskan sea otter was being discussed.

Now there are sea otter in the waters around the Queen Charlotte Islands: not many, but they can be seen by anyone who takes the time to watch the offshore kelp beds. The "sirens of the sea" are what Marius Barbeau called the sea otter in an article written more than 50 years ago. In the same piece he wrote that "The discovery of the sea otter, and the resultant China trade...led to a fresh outlook on world affairs." [12] Today the return of the sea otter, like the creation of the World Heritage Site at Ninstints and the Gwaii Haanas/South Moresby Park Reserve, is the result of another "fresh outlook on world affairs".

Just east of sundown, history has been turned around in the Queen Charlotte Islands. It is a place the Haida are proud to call home.

SOME PLACE NAMES

Aero, Gillatt Arm. The name is derived from aeroplane spruce.

Alliford Bay, southeast shore of Skidegate Inlet. Captain Daniel Pender named this location after William Alliford, the coxswain of the boat carrying the crew that sounded the bay in 1866.

Anthony Island, an island west of Kunghit Island. Site of the Haida village of Ninstints. Named in honour of Archdeacon Anthony Denny of Ardfert, Ireland, father of a midshipman aboard HMS *Virago* in 1853.

Barry Inlet, between Murray Cove and Mike Inlet, west coast of Moresby Island. Captain B. Barry served as mate for Captain Absolom Freeman of the halibut schooner *New England*.

Beattie Anchorage, northwest coast of Louise Island. George D. Beattie was an early settler on Graham Island.

Benjamin Point, small point off southeast coast of Moresby Island. Named by George Dawson after William Benjamin Carpenter, an English naturalist.

Beresford Bay, outside coast of Graham Island north of Frederick Island. William Beresford was here in 1787.

Buck Point, at the outside mouth of Buck Channel, south of Chaatl Island. Supposedly honours Buck family who were well known in Norwich, a town in Captain Vancouver's home county of Norfolk.

Burnaby Island, southeast coast of Moresby south of Juan Perez Sound. Named after Robert Burnaby, a Victoria businessman, in 1862.

Cadman Island, off the southern shore of Kano Inlet, which can be reached by foot at low tide. Richard Cadman Etches was a British businessman who helped found the King George's Sound Company in 1786. This was the company that sent the *Queen Charlotte* and *King George* to the Northwest Coast.

Cape Ball, 6 1/2 miles northeast of Tlell on the east coast of Graham Island. In Haida the name refers to either a sea god or a point rising to a plateau.

Cape Henry, southernmost point at entrance to Englefield Bay; west coast of Moresby Island. Sir Henry Englefield was a friend of Vancouver's.

Cape Knox, northwest tip of Graham Island. In 1853 Henry Needham Knox was a mate aboard the HMS *Virago*.

Carew Bay, southern shore of Kano Inlet with sheltered waters and two mooring buoys; west coast of Moresby Island. The first mate on the *Queen Charlotte* was John Ewen Carew.

Carpenter Bay, between Benjamin Point and Rankine Islands, east coast of Moresby Island. See Benjamin Point.

Cartwright Sound, southwest coast of Graham Island. Named by Vancouver to honour John Cartwright, a British naval officer and political figure.

Celestial Bluff, north coast of Port Chanal; west coast Graham Island. Named after the *Celestial Empire*, a halibut schooner.

Christie River, flows into Virago Sound. Origin of the name is unknown; the Haida called it Grizzly Bear River, which probably refers to the mythological sea bear.

Coates Creek, empties into Port Louis. John A. Coates was a hunter and prospector on the islands, around 1900.

Dana Inlet, eight miles long and a mile wide, opens into Laskeek Bay. James Dwight Dana was an American archeologist; this inlet was named after him by George Dawson in 1878.

Darwin Sound, separates east coast of Moresby Island and Lyell Island. Dawson named it in honour of Charles Darwin.

Deena Creek, flows into South Bay; south of Sandilands Island, Skidegate Inlet. Derived from an unknown Haida word.

Delkatla Wildlife Preserve, at Masset. Delkatla was a townsite in 1911 and is now part of Masset; apparently Delkatla comes from a Haida name for the slough and flats here.

Dodge Point, northeast coast of Lyell Island. In 1948, for unknown reasons, this point was named after Josiah Dodge, a sailor who served aboard the *Columbia* in 1787.

Dolomite Narrows, locally known as Burnaby Narrows; central portion of Burnaby Strait, between Burnaby and Moresby islands. Named after the mineral by Dawson.

Eden Lake, site of logging operations in the 1970s; head of Naden Harbour. As this lake is on the Naden River, Eden may be a corrupt version of the river's name.

Englefield Bay, only partially surveyed; west coast of Moresby west of Hibben Island. See Cape Henry.

Faraday Island, seemingly separated from Murchison Island by Cogit Passage, but this passage is blocked by rocks; between Lyell and Ramsey islands. Named by Dawson to honour Michael Faraday, the British scientist.

Flamingo Inlet, 5 1/2 miles long and rocky; southwest coast of Moresby Island. Named by Captain Freeman for a steam trawler. See Barry Inlet.

Flower Pot Island, with its domed profile sits in the entrance of Logan Inlet; north coast of Tanu Island; once the location of Haida fortifications. Dawson was reminded of flowers growing out of a pot due to trees and the island's shape.

Frederick Island, rocky and heavily wooded; separated from the west coast of Graham Island by a narrow passage; between Beresford and Athlow bays. Named in honour of Frederick Ingraham by his uncle Captain Joseph Ingraham.

Goski Bay, a poor anchorage in Gowgaia Bay. This is the Anglicized name of a Haida village that once stood here.

Graham Island. Named for Sir James Robert Graham, a British politician.

Gray Bay, east coast of Moresby Island south of Sandspit to which it is connected by road. Possibly named by Dawson to honour Captain Robert Gray.

Hancock River, empties into Masset Harbour. John Hancock was a signer of the US Declaration of Independence and the *Hancock* was a ship named in his honour; her master, Captain Samuel Crowell, named Masset Sound Hancock's River. In 1907 the river was given the name.

Heater Harbour, sheltered anchorage with mooring buoy; south of Rose Harbour, Kunghit Island. William Heater was a sealer and whaler who sometimes worked in these waters.

Hecate Strait, separates Queen Charlotte Islands and BC mainland. Named in honour of the HMS *Hecate*, a paddle-wheel sloop, originally intended as a survey vessel.

Hibben Island, 8 miles long; east coast of Englefield Bay. Named for Thomas Napier Hibben, an American who opened one of Victoria's first bookstores in 1858.

Hiellen River, empties into McIntyre Bay. Sometime around 1860 warriors from the Nass River burned the town of Hiellen or, more properly, Tlielang, to the ground.

Hosu Cove, rock-strewn indentation on the northern coast of Athlow Bay; west coast of Graham Island. Hosu is the Anglicized version of an unknown Haida name for this cove.

Houston Stewart Channel, separates Moresby and Kunghit islands. Commander William Houston Stewart was the first commander of the HMS *Virago*.

Howe Bay, east coast of Kunghit Island. Lieutenant Richard S. Howe served aboard the *Columbia* in 1787-1790.

Hunter Point, entrance of Cartwright Sound. Named in honour of Dr. John Hunter by his friend and patient, Captain George Vancouver.

Huxley Island, north coast of Burnaby Island, Juan Perez Sound. Named by Dawson to commemorate the life and work of Darwin's and Lyell's friend, Thomas Henry Huxley.

Ian Lake, the islands' largest lake, drains into north coast of Masset Inlet. Corruption of the original Haida name.

Ingraham Bay, west coast of Graham Island south of Frederick Island. After Joseph Ingraham, captain of the *Hope*.

Inskip Channel, north coast of Hibben Island. After George Inskip, master of the HMS *Virago* in 1853.

Jalun River, empties into Dixon Entrance. George Dawson's version of an unknown Haida word.

Jedway, Harriet Harbour, Skincuttle Inlet. From a Haida term supposedly meaning a snare or the throat of a fish trap.

Joseph Rocks, outside Ingraham Bay; west coast of Graham Island. Named for Joseph Ingraham, captain of the *Hope*.

Kunghit Island, largest island southeast of Moresby Island. This is the island's Haida name, which may mean "to the south".

Langara Island, also known as North Island, north of Graham Island. Don Juan de Langara was an admiral in the Spanish navy.

Louise Island, 13 miles long, 11 wide; east coast of Moresby Island. Princess Louise was Queen Victoria's fourth daughter.

Louscoone Inlet, south side of Moresby Island. The Haida term for a good or fine point.

Lyell Island, 11 miles long, 10 wide; east coast of Moresby Island. Named by Dawson to honour the geologist Sir Charles Lyell.

McLean Fraser Point, the centre of a largely unsurveyed area; north of Flamingo Inlet, west coast of Graham Island. Fraser was a biology professor at the University of British Columbia.

Mayer Lake, east of Port Clements in Naikoon Provincial Park. George Hardy Mayer settled locally in 1907.

Mitchell Inlet, only partially surveyed; one of several inlets on south coast of Englefield Bay. Captain William Mitchell was employed by the HBC.

Moresby Island, second largest of the Queen Charlotte Islands. Honours Sir Fairfax Moresby, a British admiral.

Naden Harbour, north coast of Graham Island, head of Virago Sound. Perhaps a Haida term that refers to the many towns once on the shores of this harbour.

Pacofi Bay, opens east into Dana Passage and Selwyn Inlet. Refers to the Pacific Fish Company, which operated a cannery in the area.

Port Clements. Named after Herbert Clements, an MP with no local connections.

Rankine Islands, group of small islands at entrance to Carpenter Bay. Rankine Dawson was George Dawson's youngest brother.

Rennell Sound, west coast of Graham Island. Possibly after James Rennell, a British geographer at the time Dixon was in the area.

Richardson Island, lies in Richardson Passage, which separates Lyell and Tanu islands. The geologist James Richardson was in the area in 1872.

Rose Harbour, locality at north end of Kunghit Island. George Rose was an 18th-century British writer and politician.

San Christoval Range, west coast of Moresby Island. Named Los Cerros de San Cristobal—St. Christopher's Peaks—by Perez.

Selwyn Inlet, east coast of Moresby Island, south of Louise Island. Honours A.R.C. Selwyn, one-time director of the Geological Survey of Canada.

Tanu Island, north of Lyell Island. Tanu is a Haida word for eel grass.

Tar Islands, east coast of Lyell Island. Named due to report that a tar-like substance is secreted by the rocks on these islands.

Tasu Sound, west coast of Moresby Island. Based on a Haida term meaning Lake of Food Inlet.

Tian Head, between Ingraham Bay and Port Louis. The name in Haida refers to the good seal hunting in the area.

Tlell. A Haida word whose meaning has been forgotten, but which may have referred to either the local berries or the surf.

Yakoun River, empties into Yakoun Bay, Masset Inlet. Apparently the original Haida word was a geographical term.

Yakulanas Bay, southern portion of Gowgaia Bay. Name of a long-deserted Haida village.

Ellipses (...) have not always been used to indicate the omission of a word or phrase, line or paragraph, from a quotation when the omission (s) did not alter the author's meaning. *Sic* has not been used in quotes to confirm the accuracy of idiosyncratic or obsolete spelling.

INTRODUCTION: THE CALL OF THE ISLANDS
1. Hedgpeth, p. 99.
2. Kelsey, p. 43.
3. *Ibid.*, p. 44.
4. *Ibid.*, p. 44.

CHAPTER ONE: CEREMONIAL TIME
1. Jenness, p. 333.
2. McFeat, pp. 4-5.
3. De Laguna, p. 30.
4. Hydrographic Office, p. 511.
5. Howay, *Voyages of the Columbia*, pp. 97-98.
6. Duff and Kew, p.7.
7. Lillard, *Ghostland People*, p. 127.
8. Barbeau, *Totem Poles*, vol. 1, p. 5.
9. Lillard, *Ghostland People*, pp. 127-8.
10. Lillard, *Wake of the War Canoe*, p. 156.
11. *Ibid.*, pp. 38-9.
12. *Ibid.*, pp. 53-4.
13. *Ibid.*, p. 54.

CHAPTER TWO: SPIRIT HELPERS AND PROCLAMATIONS OF PRESTIGE
1. Lillard, *Wake of the War Canoe*, pp. 141-2.
2. Lillard, *Ghostland People*, pp. 163-4.
3. James Joyce, *A Portrait of the Artist as a Young Man*, p. 253.
4. Deans, pp. 8-9.
5. Poole, pp. 146-7.
6. Lillard, *Ghostland People*, pp. 297-8.
7. Swanton, p. 111.
8. Reid, pp. 90-1.
9. Frazer, from Totemism and Exogamy, quoted in *Standard Dictionary of Folklore, Mythology and Legend*, p. 1120.
10. "The Totem from Tanoo," a one-page information sheet distributed by the Ethnology Division, British Columbia Provincial Museum.

CHAPTER THREE: WHERE HISTORY AND GEOGRAPHY COLLIDE
1. Crespi, pp. 157-61.
2. Campbell, pp. 91-7; see also Lillard, *Ghostland People*, pp. 48- 54.
3. Stephen, p. v.
4. Wagner, p. 187.
5. Stephen, p. v.
6. Reid, p. 9.
7. Quoted in unidentified MS, apparently by Bruce McKelvie; collection of author.
8. Davies, p. 257.
9. Quoted in unidentified MS, apparently by Bruce McKelvie; collection of author.
10. See Campbell above.
11. Poole, pp. 266-98.
12. Lillard, "Was First Man A Polynesian?" *Times-Colonist*, N.d
13. Swanton, pp. 327-29.

CHAPTER FOUR: THESE FORTUNATE ISLANDS
1. Howay, *Voyages of the Columbia*, pp. 97-8.
2. See Cook, pp. 58-9; Beals pp. 24-7.
3. Pena, pp. 159-61.
4. Beals, pp. 52-53; Pena, p. 165.
5. Beresford, pp. 220-30.
6. Walbran, p. 145.
7. Howay, "Indian Attacks...," pp. 288-9.
8. Howay, *Voyages of the Columbia*, p. 379.

9. Howay, "Indian Attacks...," p. 292.
10. Howay, "The Ballad of the Bold Northwest Man...," pp. 115-17.
11. Howay, "Indian Attacks...," pp. 297-8.
12. *Ibid.*, p. 298.
13. Vancouver, p. 1396.
14. Howay, *Voyages of the Columbia*, p. 200.
15. Wagner and Newcombe, pp. 213-4.
16. Cleveland, pp. 105-8.

CHAPTER FIVE: EUROPE CASTS ITS SHADOW
1. Jackman, pp. 99-101.
2. Reynolds, p. 142.
3. Scouler, p. 191; Lillard, *Ghostland People*, pp. 80-1.
4. Lillard, *Ancient Warriors*, pp. 48-62.
5. Dee, in Work, p. 40.
6. Lillard, "King of the Hydah," *Times-Colonist*, N.d.
7. Bowsfield, p. 113.
8. Rickard, "The Discovery of Gold in B.C.," p. 47.
9. Bowsfield, p. 251.
10. Rickard, "Indian Participation in the Gold Discoveries," p. 8.
11. Downie, p. 211.
12. Sage, p. 177.
13. Lillard, *Wake of the War Canoe*, pp. 71-2.
14. Unidentified newspaper article, in scrapbook, collection of author.
15. Gough, p. 103.

CHAPTER SIX: VISITORS, MISSIONARIES AND GHOSTS
1. Poole, p. 67.
2. *Ibid.*, p. 158, pp. 194-5.
3. Lillard, *Ghostland People*, p. 113.
4. *Ibid.*, pp. 115-6.
5. *Ibid.*, pp. 119-22.
6. *Ibid.*, pp. 151-52.
7. *Ibid.*, pp. 165-6.
8. Drew and Wilson, p. 195.
9. Lillard, *Wake of the War Canoe*, p. 68.
10. Morley, pp. 27-9.
11. Lillard, *Wake of the War Canoe*, pp. 80-1.
12. Lillard, *Ghostland People*, p. 196.
13. Van der Brink, pp. 95-6.

14. Lillard, *Ghostland People*, p. 143.
15. Chittenden, pp. 68-9.
16. Copy from dustjacket, Douglas Cole's *Captured Heritage*.
17. C.F. Newcombe, from unpaginated MS, collection of author.
18. Carr, p. 31.

CHAPTER SEVEN: THEY CAME TO STAY
1. Bureau of Provincial Information, 1913, pp. 92-3.
2. Van der Brink, p. 133.
3. Commission of Conservation, p. 191.
4. Hatt, pp. 38-9.
5. Mayol, *The Talking Totem Pole*, pp. 13-4.
6. Mayol to M.N. Hincks, private letter, collection of author.
7. Hedgpeth, p. 106.
8. Provincial Archives, *Queen Charlotte Islands*, p. 65.
9. Hedgpeth, pp. 105-8.

CHAPTER EIGHT: HAIDA GWAII
1. Locke, p. 8.
2. Bureau of Economics and Statistics, p. 463.
3. *Regional Index*, 1989, p. 371.
4. *Ibid.*, p. 370.
5. Ministry of Economic Development, p. 409.
6. *Ibid.*, p. 409.
7. Locke, p. 14.
8. Van der Brink, p. 179.
9. Reid, *Out of the Silence*, p. 90.
10. B.C. Parks, p. 19.
11. Islands Protection poster, collection of author.
12. Barbeau, "Siren of the Seas," p. 12.

ACKNOWLEDGEMENTS AND SOURCES

Marlyn Horsdal, my editor, and Rhonda Batchelor, my wife, made this book possible. My thanks to Robin Skelton and Michael Gregson, who contributed so much to so many conversations.

BOOKS

Bancroft, Hubert Howe. *History of British Columbia* (1887)
     History of the Northwest Coast, two vols. (1884)

Barbeau, Marius. *Alaska Beckons* (1947)
     Haida Carvers in Argillite (1957)
     Haida Myths Illustrated in Argillite Carvings (1953)
     Totem Poles, two vols. (n.d.)
     Pathfinders in the North Pacific (1958)

Barrington, Daines. Trans. *Voyage of the Sonora* (1920)

Beals, Herbert K. Translation and Annotation by. *Juan Perez on the Northwest Coast* (1989)

Beresford, William. *A Voyage Around the World* (1789)

Blackman, Margaret B. *During My Time* (1982)

Boas, Franz. *Tsimshian Mythology* (1916)

Bowsfield, Hartwell. Ed. *Fort Victoria Letters*, 1846-1851 (1979)

Brett, Brian. *Fossil Ground at Phantom Creek* (1976)

BC Department of Mines. *Placer-Mining in British Columbia* (1931)

BC Parks. Ministry of Environment, Lands and Parks. *Naikoon Park: Master Plan Background Document* (1992)

Brooks, Charles Wolcott. *Japanese Wrecks* (1876)

Brown, A. Sutherland. *Geology of the Queen Charlotte Islands* (1968)

Bureau of Economics and Statistics. *Regional Index of British Columbia* (1966)

Bureau of Provincial Information. *New British Columbia, The Undeveloped Areas of the Great Central and Northern Interior* (1910) *New British Columbia, The Undeveloped Areas of the Great Central and Northern Interior* (1913)

Calder, James A. and Roy L. Taylor. *Flora of the Queen Charlotte Islands*, Part 1 (1968)

Canada, Geographic Board. *Handbook of Indians of Canada* (1912)

Carey, Neil G. *A Guide to the Queen Charlotte Islands* (1975)

Carr, Emily. *The Emily Carr Omnibus* (1993)

Carter, Anthony. *This is Haida* (1968)

Chittenden, Newton H. *Official Report of the Exploration of the Queen Charlotte Islands* (1884)

Cleveland, Richard Jeffry. *Voyages and Commercial Enterprises* (n.d.)

Cogo, Robert. *Haida Food Gathering and Preparation* (n.d.) *Haida Months of the Year* (1979) *Haida Story Telling Time* (1979)

Commission of Conservation. *Tenth Annual Report* (1919)

Cook, Warren L. *Floodtide of Empire* (1973)

Dalzell, Kathleen E. *The Queen Charlotte Islands, 1774-1966* (1968)
The Queen Charlotte Islands, Of Places and Names (1973)

Davies, Nigel. *Voyagers to the New World* (1979)

Dawson, George M. *Notes and Observations on the Qwakiool People of the Northern Part of Vancouver Island and of the Adjacent Coasts* (1887)

Deans, James. *Tales from the Totems of Hidery* (1899)

De Laguna, Frederica. *The Story of a Tlingit Community* (1960)

Downie, William. *Hunting for Gold* (1893)

Drew, Leslie and Douglas Wilson. *Argillite Art of the Haida* (1980)

Drucker, Philip. *Cultures of the North Pacific Coast* (1965)

Duff, Wilson. *The Indian History of British Columbia* (1964)

Fladmark, Knut R. *British Columbia Prehistory* (1986)

Foster, J.B. *The Evolution of the Mammals of the Queen Charlotte Islands* (1965)

Gough, Barry M. *Gunboat Frontier* (1984)

Halpin, Marjorie M. *Totem Poles* (1981)

Harris, Christie. *Raven's Cry* (1992)

Hatt, D.E. *Sitka Spruce* (1919)

Hedgpeth, Joel W. *The Outer Shores*, Part One (1978)

Heyerdahl, Thor. *American Indians in the Pacific* (1952)

Holland, Stuart S. *Landforms of British Columbia* (1964)

Howay, Frederic W. Ed. *Voyages of the Columbia* (1990)
   Ed. Richard A. Pierce. *A List of the Trading Vessels in the Maritime Fur Trade, 1785-1825* (1941)

Hydrographic Office, Admiralty. *The British Columbia Pilot* (1888)

Ingraham, Joseph. Ed. Mark D. Kaplanoff. *Voyage to the Northwest Coast of North America, 1790-92* (1971)

Islands Protection Society. *Islands at the Edge* (1984)

Jackman, S.W. Ed. *The Journal of William Sturgis* (1978)

Jenness, Diamond. *The Indians of Canada* (1977)

Kelsey, Vera. *British Columbia Rides a Star* (1958)

La Perouse, Jean Francois de Galaup, Comte de. *A Voyage Around the World* (1799)

Lillard, Charles. *Seven Shillings a Year* (1986)
   Ed. *In the Wake of the War Canoe* (1981)
   Warriors of the North Pacific (1984)
   Ghostland People (1989)

McDonald, George. *Chiefs of the Sea and Sky* (1989)
   Ninstints (1983).

McDonald, Lucile. *Swan Among the Indians* (1972)

McFeat, Tom. *Indians of the North Pacific* (1966)

Marchand, Etienne. *A Voyage Around the World* (1801)

Mayol, Lurline Bowles. *The Talking Totem Pole* (1930)
   The Big Canoe (1933)

Meares, John. *Voyages Made in the Year 1788 and 1789* (1790)

Mertz, Henriette. *Gods from the Far East: How the Chinese Discovered America* (1972)

Morley, Alan. *Roar of the Breakers* (1967)

Musgrave, Susan. *The Charcoal Burners* (1980)

Newton, Norman. *Fire in the Raven's Nest* (1973)

Niblack, Albert P. *Coast Indians of Southern Alaska and Northern British Columbia* (1888)

Pielou, E.C. *After the Ice Age* (1991)

Plummer, Katherine. *The Shogun's Reluctant Ambassadors* (1991)

Poole, Francis. *Queen Charlotte Islands* (1872)

Province of British Columbia. *The Prince Rupert-Smithers Bulletin* (1967)
Ministry of Economic Development. *British Columbia Regional Index* (1986) and (1989)

Ministry of Finance and Corporate Relations. *British Columbia Economic and Statistical Review* (1989)

Provincial Archives. *Haida* (1952)
    Queen Charlotte Islands (1953)

Reid, Bill. *Out of the Silence* (1971)
    and Robert Bringhurst. *The Raven Steals the Light* (1984)

Reynolds, Stephen. Ed. F.W. Howay. *The Voyage of the New Hazard* (1970)

Roe, M. Ed. *The Journals and Letters of Captain Charles Bishop* (1967)

Sage, Walter N. *Sir James Douglas and British Columbia* (1930)

Sheldon, Charles. *The Wilderness of the North Pacific Coast Islands* (1912)

Smyly, John and Carolyn Smyly. *Those Born at Koona* (1973)

South Moresby Resource Planning Team. *South Moresby: Land Use Alternatives* (1981)

Stephen, A.M. *The Kingdom of the Sun* (1927)

Suttles, Wayne. *Handbook of the North American Indians: The Northwest Coast* (1990)

Swanton, John R. *Haida Texts and Myths* (1905)

Thornton, Mildred Valley. *Indian Lives and Legends* (1966)

Turner, W.O. *Call the Beast thy Brother* (1973)

Vancouver, George. Ed. W. Kaye Lamb. *The Voyage of George Vancouver 1791-1795*, four vols. (1984)

Van der Brink, J.H. *The Haida Indians: Cultural Change Mainly Between 1876-1970* (1974)

Virgo, Sean. *Deathwatch on Skidegate Narrows and Other Poems* (1979)

Wagner, H.R. *Apocryphal Voyages to the Northwest Coast of America* (1932)

Walbran, Captain John T. *British Columbia Coast Names* (1971)

Work, John. Introduction and notes by Henry Drummond Dee. *The Journal of John Work* (1945)

Yates, J. Michael. *Insel, The Queen Charlotte Islands Meditations* (1983)

MISCELLANEOUS

Anonymous. "Primary Industries," *News Herald*, April 1941.

Barbeau, Marius. "Siren of the Seas," *The Beaver*, December 1944.

Campbell, John. "The Origin of the Haidahs of the Queen Charlotte Islands," The Royal Society of Canada. *Proceedings and Transactions*, Series 2, Vol. 3, Section 2, 1897-98.

Clapp, C.H. "A Geological Reconnaissance on Graham Island....," G.S.C. *Report of Progress*, 1914.

Crespi, Fray. "Journal of Fray Crespi," *Sutro Collection*, Doc. 19, 1891.

Cullins, James. "The Queen Charlotte Islands," *British Columbia Magazine*, December 1913.

Duff, Wilson and Michael Kew. "Anthony Island," Annual Report of the Provincial Museum of British Columbia, 1958.

Elliott, G.R.B. "Graham Island," *British Columbia Magazine*, March and April 1912.

Ells, R.W. "Report on Graham Island....," G.S.C. *Report*, New Series, Vol. XVI, 1904.

Harrington, Lyn. "The Queen Charlotte Islands," *Canadian Geographic*, Vol. 39, No. 2.

Haynes, Bessie Doak. "Gold on Queen Charlotte's Island," *The Beaver*, Winter 1966.

Howay, F.W. "The Ballad of the Bold Northwestman: An Incident in the Life of Captain John Kendrick," *The Washington Historical Quarterly*, April 1929.
    "Early Days of the Maritime Fur-Trade on the Northwest Coast," *The Canadian Historical Review*, Vol. 4.
    "Indian Attacks Upon Maritime Fur Traders of the North-West Coast, 1785-1805," *The Canadian Historical Review*, Vol. 6.
    "The Voyage of the 'Captain Cook' and the 'Experiment', 1785-86," *British Columbia Historical Quarterly*, Vol. 5, No. 4.
    "The Voyage of the Hope: 1790-1792," *The Washington Historical Quarterly*, Vol. XI, No. 1.
    "A Yankee Trader on the Northwest Coast, 1791-1795," *The Washington Historical Quarterly*, Vol. 21.

Lillard, Charles. "Time Before Time," *Horizon Canada*, Vol. 1, No. 1.

Locke, Jeannine. "The Haidas", *Canadian Weekly*, n.d.

MacKenzie, J.D. "Geology of Graham Island," G.S.C. *Memoir 88*, 1916.

Newcombe, C.F. "Notes of a Journey Round the Southern Islands of the Queen Charlotte Group, British Columbia in the Year 1901," copy of typed MS, held by C. Lillard.

Newcombe, W.A. "A Brief History of the Queen Charlotte Islands," Fourth Report and Proceedings, British Columbia Historical Association, 1929.

Pena, Fray Tomas de la. "Journal of Fray Tomas de la Pena," *Sutro Collection*, Doc. 18, 1891.

Rickard, T.A. "The Discovery of Gold in B.C.," *The Beaver*, March 1942.
  "Indian Participation in the Gold Discoveries," *British Columbia Historical Quarterly*, January 1938.

Scouler, Dr. John. "Journal of a Voyage to NW America", unidentified magazine article, held by C. Lillard.

Wagner, H.R. and W.A. Newcombe. "The Journal of Jacinto Caamano," *British Columbia Historical Quarterly*, July 1938.